1974

This book may be kept

# Spinoza's Metaphysics

Spinoza's Metaphysics: An Essay

in Interpretation    by E. M. Curley

*Harvard University Press, Cambridge, Massachusetts, 1969*

To Ruth

We dance round in a ring and suppose,
But the Secret sits in the middle and knows.

                                Robert Frost*

* From *Complete Poems of Robert Frost*. Copyright 1942 by Robert Frost.
Reprinted by permission of Holt, Rinehart and Winston, Inc.

A philosopher's real power over mankind resides not in his metaphysical formulas, but in the spirit and tendencies which have led him to adopt those formulas. Spinoza's critic has, therefore, rather to bring to light that spirit and those tendencies of his author than to exhibit his metaphysical formulas. Propositions about substance pass by mankind at large like the idle wind, which mankind at large regards not; it will not even listen to a word about those propositions, unless it first learns what their author was driving at with them, and finds that this object of his is one with which it sympathises, one, at any rate, which commands its attention.

—Matthew Arnold, *Essays in Criticism,* "Spinoza and the Bible"

# Preface

Spinoza, in the three hundred years since he lived and wrote, has been praised and damned for a most amazing variety of intellectual virtues and vices. Damnation came first. The verdict of his Christian contemporaries was that in identifying God with Nature he was guilty of atheism, and consequently his major work, the *Ethics,* could not prudently be published during his lifetime. On the other hand, his co-religionists of the Jewish community in Amsterdam cast him out, not for disbelief in God, but for the heterodox opinion that God is corporeal. Nor was it only the orthodox who cried "Heretic!" As Heinrich Heine observes,

> The most opposite parties arrayed themselves against Spinoza. The aspect of this army of adversaries is highly amusing. Near a swarm of black and white Capuchins bearing cross and censer, marches the phalanx of the Encyclopedists, who also take aim at this "daring thinker"; by the side of the Rabbi of the synagogue of Amsterdam, who sounds the attack with the sacred buck's-horn, advances Arouet de Voltaire, playing obligato on the shrill pipe of irony for the benefit of deism.[1]

No doubt there was an ulterior motive in the Voltaire-Bayle disparagement of Spinoza as an atheist. Both clearly relished the notion that the most heretical of doctrines may be espoused by a man of unimpeachable character. For their purpose, they needed a Spinoza who was a blank, frank atheist.

In a somewhat similar way, Spinoza's "universal infamy" as an atheist served Hume's purpose when he attempted to show an identity between the popular doctrine that the soul is an immaterial substance and the "hideous hypothesis" that there is only one substance. To show that a thesis reduced to Spinozism was, in the eighteenth century, a very serious criticism. But this only illustrates the esteem in which Spinoza was generally held.

Contrast this nearly unanimous condemnation of Spinoza prior to, say, 1780, with the treatment accorded him since. We find Heine claiming that "nothing but sheer unreason and malice could bestow on such a doctrine the qualification of atheism—no one has ever spoken more sublimely of Deity than Spinoza," and Ernest Renan crediting him with "the truest vision ever had of God." We find the liberal Protestant theologian Friedrich Schleiermacher writing of the "holy and excommunicated Spinoza" and the Catholic poet Novalis coining the famous phrase "the God-intoxicated man" in his honor.

If, prior to 1780, the most opposite parties arrayed themselves against Spinoza, since then the situation has reversed itself, and people of the most diverse interests and temperaments have seen in him a sympathizer. He is at once a pantheistic mystic, whose closest spiritual cousin is the Buddha, and the last of the medieval Jewish philosophers, whose philosophic kinship is to Moses Maimonides, Chasdai Crescas, and Aristotle. While the Marxists have claimed him as a precursor of dialectical materialism, H. H. Joachim and others have viewed him as expounding a form of absolute idealism. Friedrich Nietzsche, when he discovered Spinoza, immediately wrote an excited postcard to Franz Overbeck, proclaiming that at last he had found a predecessor: "Not only is his over-all tendency like mine—making knowledge the *most powerful* affect—but in five main points of his doctrine I recognize myself . . . he denies the freedom of the will, teleology, the moral world order, the unegoistic and evil."[2] C. S. Peirce regarded Spinoza as one of the three forerunners of pragmatism, though John Wild says confidently that the pragmatic theory of truth would have appeared absurd to Spinoza. And most recently he has been interpreted by Stuart Hampshire as a philosopher of science on the grand scale, giving metaphysical expression, within a fundamentally Cartesian framework, to the ideal of a unified science.

In the face of such diversity of opinion, one hesitates to add to the confusion. Nevertheless, I feel that I have something to contribute to the understanding of Spinoza, and for better or for worse I will have my say. My method, contrary to Matthew Arnold's perfectly sensible advice, will be to begin by trying to show how Spinoza's metaphysical formulas are to be construed. I do not think we can profitably discuss his spirit and tendencies until we have some idea of what the formulas mean. No doubt we must approach them tentatively, keeping in mind the possibility of other interpretations, and no doubt our choice of interpretations to try out must be guided by some hypotheses about his spirit and tendencies. But in the end we must come back to the text, and it seems to me just as well to begin there. Those impatient souls who must know what my conclusions are before they learn the reasons for them may do what they would do if this were a detective story: turn to the end of the book.

My main concern is to provide the most coherent and precise explanation I can of the fundamental propositions of Spinoza's metaphysics. To do this I will make use of a philosophical vocabulary which was entirely unfamiliar to Spinoza. I do not contend that Spinoza thought in these terms. I do contend that his philosophy can be expressed in these terms with remarkable success. The measure of success here is whether or not we can, in the language suggested, make connections between the various things Spinoza says and show him to have a consistent, reasoned view of the world. If this can be done, I shall consider the use of these admittedly alien categories to be justified.

I have said that my primary aim has been understanding. I should perhaps add that, if my understanding has been correct, many of the criticisms usually directed against Spinoza are seriously misguided. To that extent, my interpretation of Spinoza will also be a defense of Spinoza.

Translations are my own, unless otherwise indicated. Those of Spinoza's works are done from the critical edition of Carl Gebhardt. I have quoted freely from works other than the *Ethics,* and this is perhaps the place to comment on the relative authority of these works. Briefly, my position is that no work other than the *Ethics* and perhaps the later letters in the *Correspondence* is fully satisfactory as a source for the views of the mature Spinoza. The *Metaphysical Thoughts* and

*Descartes' Principles of Philosophy* are both, in part at any rate, expositions of the views of Descartes, though I believe they contain important
indications of Spinoza's own views. Suspicion has been plausibly cast
on the *Theological-Political Treatise* on the ground that there Spinoza
is accommodating himself to the opinions of the vulgar in order to make
his message more acceptable. The *Political Treatise* is an unfinished
work, as are the *Short Treatise* (*on God, Man and his Well-Being*)
and the *Treatise* (*on the Correction of the Intellect*). Both of these
latter works, moreover, are early and show significant differences on
some points from the final teaching of the *Ethics*. But after all reserva-
tions have been made, these other works still remain valuable sources
for the study of Spinoza. I think there is no good reason not to appeal
to them so long as the passage cited is not inconsistent with the *Ethics*.
When the passage has seemed to me inconsistent with the teaching of
the *Ethics* I have generally indicated this.

There are a number of people and institutions to whom I should
here express my appreciation for the contribution they have made to
my writing of this book: first, Professor Bernard Peach, who supervised
my work when it was a doctoral dissertation at Duke University, and
who gave of his time, energy, and wisdom to an extent that was surely
beyond the requirements of duty; Professor Romane Clark, whose comments on the various visions and revisions of the manuscript were always
incisive; the Graduate School of Arts and Sciences at Duke, for the
generous fellowship which made my study there possible; my fellow
students in Professor Peach's Spinoza seminar, who provided much of
the stimulus for the ideas expressed here; the Institute of Advanced
Studies of the Australian National University, for giving me the opportunity to rethink and rewrite my earlier work under conditions as nearly
ideal as one may hope for in an imperfect world; Professor John Passmore, whose kind advice and criticism have been most helpful; Mrs.
Amelie Rorty, who read this book in manuscript for the Harvard University Press and made some very useful suggestions; and finally, my

wife Ruth, without whose moral support this book would certainly never have been finished as soon as it was, and might never have been finished at all.

Canberra, Australia                                    E.M.C.
February 1969

# Contents

# Works Cited in Shortened Form

## SPINOZA'S WORKS

E     *Ethics,* ed. Carl Gebhardt. Heidelberg: Carl Winter, 1925 ($E$ I$_{A2}$ = part I, axiom 2; $E$ IIP33c = part II, proposition 33, corollary; $E$ IVP14s = part IV, proposition 14, scholium; $E$ I$_{D3}$ = part I, definition 3; $E$ IP11D3 = part I, proposition 11, demonstration 3).

TdIE     *Tractatus de Intellectus Emendatione* (*TdIE,* 76, II:29 = Bruder edition, section 76, Gebhardt edition, volume II, page 29).

KV     *Korte Verhandeling van God, de Mensch, en des zelfs Welstand* (*KV* I, ii, I:19 = part I, chapter ii, Gebhardt edition volume I, page 19).

PP     *Renati Des Cartes Principia Philosophiae.*

CM     *Cogitata Metaphysica* (*CM* I, iii, I:243 = part I, chapter iii, Gebhardt edition volume I, page 243).

Ep.     *Epistolae* (*Ep.* 21, IV:127 = Epistle 21, Gebhardt edition volume IV, page 127).

TTP     *Tractatus Theologico-Politicus.*

TP     *Tractatus Politicus.*

NS     *Nagelate Schriften.* Gebhardt's edition gives variant readings from the *Nagelate Schriften,* the Dutch translation of Spinoza's works, which appeared in 1677 at the same time as the *Opera Posthuma.* The *Nagelate Schriften* were translated from Spinoza's own manuscripts, but apparently from manuscripts which represent, in some cases, an earlier draft. They therefore provide not only a valuable check on the proofreading of the editors of the *Opera Posthuma,* but also an indication of Spinoza's final revisions.

## OTHER WORKS

Adam and Tannery     René Descartes. *Oeuvres,* ed. Charles Adam and Paul Tannery. 12 vols. Paris: J. Vrin, 1897–1913.

Arnauld and Nicole     Antoine Arnauld and Pierre Nicole. *La Logique, ou L'Art de Penser,* ed. Pierre Clair and François Girbal. Paris: Presses Universitaires de France, 1965.

Bayle

Pierre Bayle. *Historical and Critical Dictionary Selections,* trans. and ed. Richard H. Popkin. Indianapolis: Bobbs-Merrill, 1965.

Caird

John Caird. *Spinoza.* London: Wm. Blackwood and Sons, 1907.

de Deugd

C. de Deugd. *The Significance of Spinoza's First Kind of Knowledge.* Assen: Van Gorcum, 1966.

Friedman

George Friedman. *Leibniz et Spinoza.* Paris: Gallimard, 1962.

Gerhardt

G. W. Leibniz. *Die philosophischen Schriften,* ed. C. J. Gerhardt. 7 vols. Hildesheim: Georg Olm, 1960–1962.

Hampshire

Stuart Hampshire. *Spinoza.* London: Faber and Faber, 1956.

Joachim, *Study*

H. H. Joachim. *A Study of the Ethics of Spinoza.* Oxford: Clarendon Press, 1901.

Joachim, *Spinoza's Tractatus*

H. H. Joachim. *Spinoza's Tractatus de Intellectus Emendatione.* Oxford: Clarendon Press, 1940.

Lovejoy

Arthur O. Lovejoy. *The Great Chain of Being: A Study of the History of an Idea.* Cambridge, Mass.: Harvard University Press, 1936.

Pollock

Frederick Pollock. *Spinoza: His Life and Philosophy.* London: C. K. Paul, 1880; second edition, 1899. References are to the first editon, unless otherwise indicated.

Russell

Bertrand Russell. *A History of Western Philosophy.* London: Allen and Unwin, 1946.

Versfeld

Marthinus Versfeld. *An Essay on the Metaphysics of Descartes.* London: Methuen, 1940.

Wiener

*Leibniz, Selections,* ed. Philip P. Wiener. New York: Scribner, 1951.

Wolf

*Spinoza's Short Treatise on God, Man and his Well-being,* trans. and ed. A. Wolf. New York: Russell & Russell, 1963.

Wolfson

H. A. Wolfson. *The Philosophy of Spinoza: Unfolding the Latent Processes of His Reasoning.* 2 vols. Cambridge, Mass.: Harvard University Press, 1934.

Spinoza's Metaphysics

It is not true that his followers have been very numerous. Very few persons are suspected of adhering to his theory; and among those who are suspected of it, there are few who have studied it; and among the latter group, there are few who have understood it and have not been discouraged by the perplexities and the impenetrable abstractions that are found in it . . . of all the hypotheses of atheism, Spinoza's is the least capable of misleading anybody, for . . . it opposes the most distinct notions in the human mind.

—Pierre Bayle, *Dictionary,* "Spinoza"

# 1 The Definitions of Substance and Mode

We are about to plunge into waters that are very, very muddy. Many people talk with a great deal of confidence about Spinoza's philosophy. But among those who have studied it carefully, there is no general agreement on the meaning of even those doctrines that are the most central. What Bayle wrote, at the end of the seventeenth century, might be written with equal truth today. No philosopher should be easier to understand than Spinoza, for none has taken so much trouble to explain himself, defining his key terms, listing his basic assumptions, and arguing carefully for each conclusion he draws from those assumptions. But few have proved harder.

Consider the antithesis of substance and mode. That this is central to Spinoza's metaphysics is evident from the first axiom of the *Ethics,* which divides reality into substances and modes. "Everything which exists either exists in itself or exists in something else" (*E* IA1). What exists in itself, and is thus conceived through itself, is a substance (*E* ID3). What exists in something else, through which it is conceived, is a mode or affection of substance (*E* ID5). There is nothing that does not fall into one of these two categories.

But what Spinoza intends by this antithesis is not at all clear. True, he gives us, as his geometric method requires, definitions of these crucial terms. The definitions, however, are not particularly helpful. What, precisely, is Spinoza saying when he says that to be a substance a thing must exist in itself and be conceived through itself? What are we told when we are told that modes exist in something else through which they are conceived? Couched in a highly abstract, technical language, these definitions are open to a wide variety of interpretations, as three hundred years of commentary on Spinoza amply demonstrate.

In this chapter, I shall contend that two of the most widespread and plausible interpretations of Spinoza's definitions are wrong. And because the concepts of substance and mode are so central to his philosophy, this will involve arguing, as well, that many of the things often said about Spinoza—both by his critics and by people who thought they agreed with him—are mistaken. In conclusion, I shall try to indicate, in a rough way, how I think we should understand the definitions. Perhaps some of the abstractions are penetrable; perhaps some of the perplexities can be removed.

## The Bayle-Joachim Interpretation

The first of the two interpretations with which I shall deal occurs as early as Bayle's *Dictionary* and as late as Bertrand Russell's *History of Western Philosophy*. This interpretation supposes that Spinoza understood the terms "substance" and "mode" in much the same way the philosophers of the seventeenth century in general, and Descartes in particular, understood them. To see its merits and demerits, we need to begin by examining the ordinary philosophical use of these terms at that time.

Undoubtedly the seventeenth-century account of substance best known to people in the English-speaking world is Locke's, in the *Essay Concerning Human Understanding*. It is so familiar that I shall merely summarize its principal features in these five propositions:

( 1 ) A substance, in the general sense, is nothing but the subject, or substratum, in which qualitites are said to inhere, or exist, or subsist, or rest.

( 2 ) A substance *of a particular kind* is a collection or combination of qualities, together with the subject or substratum in which they all inhere.

( 3 ) The subject or substratum in which qualities inhere does not itself inhere in anything else, and hence may be said to exist or subsist by itself.

( 4 ) The subject or substratum supports and unites into one thing the qualities which inhere in it and which cannot be conceived as subsisting by themselves.

( 5 ) The subject or substratum is not perceptible to the senses; whatever we may be said to perceive through our senses is a quality. The existence of the subject, however, must be inferred from the existence of the qualities we do perceive, since the qualities cannot be conceived to subsist by themselves.[1]

Though this notion of substance as the imperceptible subject in which qualities inhere, with all the difficulties it involves for empiricism, is best known to us through Locke, it is by no means peculiar to him. It was the common property of the philosophers of the seventeenth century. Looking at the most famous logic text of that era, the *Port-Royal Logic,* we find a very similar account:

> Whatever we conceive is represented to our mind either as a thing, or as a manner of a thing, or as a modified thing.
>
> What is conceived as subsisting by itself and as the subject of all that is conceived with regard to it, I call a thing. This is what is also called a substance.
>
> I call a manner of a thing, or mode, or attribute, or quality, what, being conceived as in the thing and as not being able to subsist without it, determines it to exist in a certain way and causes it to be called such.
>
> I call it a modified thing, when we consider the substance as determined by a certain manner or mode.[2]

The Arnauld-Nicole terminology is different from Locke's. Their "thing" or "substance" is Locke's "substance in the general sense"; their "modified thing" is, roughly, Locke's "substance of a particular kind"; and where Arnauld and Nicole usually speak of a "manner" or "mode," Locke usually speaks of a "quality." But the doctrine is the same, as their example shows:

> When I consider a body, the idea which I have of it represents to me a thing or a substance, because I think of it as a thing which subsists by itself, and which has no need of any subject in order to exist.

> But when I consider that this body is round, the idea which I have
> of the roundness represents to me only a manner of being, or a
> mode, which I conceive as unable to subsist naturally without the
> body whose roundness it is.
> And, finally, when, joining the mode to the thing, I consider a
> round body, this idea represents to me a modified thing.[3]

Making allowances for merely verbal differences, nearly all of the first
four theses which I gave above as defining the Lockean concept of
substance can be duplicated from these brief passages. All that is lacking
is the doctrine that the thing in which the modes of a qualified thing
inhere is the cause of their constituting *one* thing. The fifth thesis is
suggested by a remark which comes soon afterward:

> Our mind is accustomed to know most things as modified, because
> it knows them only by the accidents or qualities which strike our
> senses. (Arnauld and Nicole, p. 47)

Arnauld and Nicole do not say what exceptions they have in mind,
but clearly the door has been left open for the kind of empiricist criticism
Locke's account received.
With Descartes, the situation is complicated by the fact that he gives
rather different definitions of substance in different places. Generally
he defines "substance" in terms of some sort of capacity for independent
existence, as in the *Principles of Philosophy:*

> When we conceive substance, we conceive only a thing which
> exists in such a way that it needs only itself in order to exist. In
> this there may be some obscurity regarding the explanation of
> this phrase "needs only itself." For properly speaking, only God
> exists in this way, and no created thing can exist for a moment
> without being sustained and conserved by his power. That is

why they are right to say in the School that the name of "substance" is not univocal with respect to God and his creatures, that is, that there is no signification of this word which we conceive distinctly which applies to him and to them. But since, among created things, some are of such a nature that they cannot exist without others, we distinguish them from those which need only the ordinary concurrence of God, calling the latter substances, and the former qualities or attributes of these substances. And the notion we thus have of created substance corresponds in the same way to all, that is, to those which are immaterial as well as to those which are material or corporeal. For in order to understand that these are substances, it is necessary only to perceive that they can exist without the aid of any created thing.[4]

Most of Descartes' other definitions of substance are variations on this theme.[5] There is in them no explicit reference to an imperceptible subject or substratum in which qualities inhere, just the notion of a capacity for independent existence, more or less strictly construed. If we had only these definitions, there might be some temptation to suppose that Descartes' concept of substance is different from Locke's, Arnauld's, and Nicole's.

In other places, however, we find Descartes giving a more clearly Lockean account of the notion of substance. When he puts into geometric form his arguments for the existence of God and the distinction of the mind from the body, he does define substance as the subject in which qualities inhere: "Every thing in which there exists immediately, as in a subject, or through which there exists, anything which we perceive, that is, any property or quality or attribute of which there is a real idea in us, is called a substance" (Adam and Tannery, VII: 161). And he goes on to explain that "We have no other idea of substance itself, precisely taken, than that it is a thing in which there exists, formally or eminently, what we perceive, or what exists objectively in some one of our ideas, because it is known by the natural light that nothing has no real attributes" (ibid.). Here it is clear enough that a substance is a subject in which qualities inhere, that it is distinct from its qualities, and that, though it is imperceptible in itself, its existence must be inferred from the existence of what we do perceive, its qualities, because they cannot exist of themselves (that is, inhere in nothing).

Indeed, Descartes is quite anxious to insist that we have no immediate knowledge of substance. This thesis is reiterated both in his reply to the objections of Hobbes and also in his reply to Arnauld.[6] And of course it is implicit in the Second Meditation, in the discussion of the piece of wax (Adam and Tannery, VII:30–34).

Thus Pierre Gassendi's empiricist criticism of Descartes on this point comes as no surprise. We may be said to have a perfect idea of a man, Gassendi remarks, if we have observed him carefully, and often, and from every angle. To the extent that we have observed him only cursorily, or not more than once, or in part, our idea will be imperfect.

> However, if we have not examined the man himself, but a mask which covers his face and clothes which conceal his body completely, then it must be said that either we have no idea of this man or, if we have any, it is most imperfect and extremely confused. Hence, I say that of accidents we have, indeed, a distinct and true idea, but of the substance lying hidden under them only a confused and extremely fictitious one. (Adam and Tannery, VII:285–286)

Descartes himself supplied the materials for this analogical argument through his use of the clothing metaphor to illustrate his conception of the relation between substance and its qualities (Adam and Tannery, VII:32, IX:35).

The distinction between substance and its qualities needs to be emphasized, because commentators on Descartes have sometimes blurred it. For example, Marthinus Versfeld, noting that there is no real distinction between substance and attribute, but only a distinction of reason, says that "substance is simply the principal attribute substantialized . . . there is nothing occult in substances, since the principal attribute, which is transparent to the understanding, constitutes their nature or essence" (Versfeld, p. 96). This seems to me most misleading. There is nothing occult in substances, except the substances themselves.

No real distinction exists between substance and attribute, because a real distinction, in Descartes' use of the term, can obtain only between two entities each of which is capable of existing apart from the other, that is, between two substances (Adam and Tannery, VIII:28–30). Where one or both of the entities is incapable of independent existence, the distinction between them must be either a distinction of reason or a modal distinction. The distinction between substance and its principal attribute, then, is only a distinction of reason because the attribute cannot be conceived as existing by itself. But it is no less a real distinction in the sense of that term in which "real" rules out "illusory."

Nowhere does Descartes indicate this more clearly than in a conversation with Frans Burman, where he comments on the definition of substance given in his geometrical presentation of the arguments for God and for the real distinction between mind and body:

> Beyond the attribute which specifies [*specificat,* a mediaevalism] substance, there must further be conceived substance itself which lies under [*substernitur*] that attribute: as, since mind is a thinking thing, there is beyond thought the substance which thinks, and so forth. (Adam and Tannery, V:156)

Substance cannot, then, be said to be simply the principal attribute substantialized.

That Descartes defines substance in two such different ways has naturally provided scholars with something of a puzzle. Why does he do this? Brunschvicg suggests that the definition in terms of existence in a subject results from the requirements of the geometric form which Descartes temporarily adopts. Created substance cannot be defined in terms of a capacity for independent existence because that would require a qualification mentioning the sustaining activity of God. But God cannot be defined prior to substance because the existence of thinking substance must be proved before the existence of God.[7]

This, however, does not seem adequate. For one thing, the fact that the qualification in the *Principles* mentions God is an accidental feature of the Latin version. In the French version this reference does not occur. For another, the first proof Descartes gives in the geometric presentation is the ontological argument, which does not depend on the prior proof of the existence of the self.

Versfeld, I think, provides the right answer. He points out that, according to Descartes, the existence of substance can be proved from the definition in terms of existence in a subject, but not from the definition in terms of a capacity for independent existence (Versfeld, p. 94). Thus, the passage quoted earlier from the *Principles* continues:

> When it is a question of knowing whether one of these substances really exists, that is, whether it is now in the world, the fact that it exists in this way [without the aid of any created thing] is not sufficient to cause us to discover it. For that alone does not disclose to us anything from which we can gain any particular knowledge. It is necessary, in addition, that it should have attributes we can observe. And any attribute will suffice for this purpose, for it is one of our common notions that nothing cannot have any attributes or properties or qualities. Hence, when we find one, we rightly conclude that it is the attribute of some substance, and that this substance exists.[8]

The definition in terms of a capacity for independent existence comes into play when Descartes' purpose is to prove, not the existence of substance, but the real distinction of the mind from the body. For if mind and body are both substances, then, by that definition, they can exist independently of one another, and so are really distinct. This, as I say, seems to me correct. I would only add that one other reason why Descartes generally preferred to define "substance" in terms of a capacity for independent existence was probably that such a definition would lead more readily to a proof of the immortality of the soul (see Adam and Tannery, IX:10).

In any case, substances have these two features for Descartes: they exist independently of everything but God, and they are the subjects in which properties inhere. Either one of these features may be taken as defining. And it is worth noting that Spinoza gives both definitions when he presents Descartes' *Principles* in geometric form.[9]

Before leaving Descartes, it should be observed that the terms "mode" and "attribute" have a rather special meaning in his thought. Both modes and attributes are properties of substance and cannot be conceived as existing apart from their subject. An attribute, however, is a very general, hence invariant, hence essential property of a substance, for example, thought, or extension. A mode, on the other hand, is a more or less specific property, hence liable to variation, hence nonessential, for example, my thinking that I exist, or roundness. Since any variableness is impossible in God, we predicate of him only attributes, not modes (Adam and Tannery, VIII:26).

I have dwelt at such length on seventeenth-century uses of the terms "substance" and "mode" partly because I wish to emphasize the naturalness of the interpretation Bayle puts on them in the long and hostile article he devotes to Spinoza in his *Dictionary*. Bayle has had his critics in recent years, but many figures of the Enlightenment accepted and repeated Bayle's criticisms of Spinoza, and it is not surprising that they should have done so.[10]

Bayle bases his objections on the attribution to Spinoza of the following doctrines:[11] (1) there is only one substance, (2) this substance is God, and (3) all finite beings are modifications of God. That Spinoza held these views, no one who is familiar with the *Ethics* can doubt.

Bayle then infers from them that God is the real subject of all propositions:

> If it were true, then, as Spinoza claims, that men are modalities of God, one would speak falsely when one said, "Peter denies this, he wants that, he affirms such and such a thing"; for actually, according to this theory, it is God who denies, wants, affirms; and consequently all the denominations that result from the thoughts of all men are properly and physically to be ascribed to God.[12]

And Bayle has no trouble showing that this view has consequences that are indeed astonishing.

Spinoza's God, he maintains, will be as changeable as the Proteus of the ancient poets, for a mutable being is merely one which, its substance remaining the same, acquires new modifications and loses those it had. Spinoza's God will be the subject of contradictory properties, for different men love and do not love, affirm and do not affirm, the same thing at the same time. These contradictory properties must be ascribed to God in violation of the laws of logic.

Moreover, all kinds of moral enormities must be predicated directly of God. We can no longer say that Brutus killed Caesar, we must say that God killed Caesar. Nor, for that matter, can we say that Caesar was killed by Brutus. We must have it that God was killed by Brutus, or rather that God killed himself. And so on, throughout a whole list of odious actions:

> All the phrases by which what men do to one another are expressed . . . have no other true sense than this, "God hates himself, he asks favors of himself and refuses them, he persecutes himself, he kills himself, he eats himself, he slanders himself, he executes himself." (Bayle, p. 312)

It is small wonder that Bayle charged Spinoza's system with being contrary to the most distinct notions of our minds.

Now it is perfectly clear that these consequences would not be acceptable to Spinoza. The immutability of God is a corollary of *E* Ip20. Spinoza's respect for the principle of contradiction seems amply indicated by his frequent use of the *reductio ad absurdum* proof technique (*E* Ip6c; *E* Ipii; *E* Ip13). As for the attribution of human sins to God, Spinoza would clearly not allow this. Evil, he writes to William de Blyenbergh, is merely a negation (*Ep.* 23), and nothing which involves negation may be attributed to God (*E* Ip8s).

The question is: Do these absurd and unacceptable consequences in fact follow from the Spinozistic doctrines Bayle says they follow from? Clearly, this depends on how we interpret the terms "substance" and "mode" and on what we conceive the relation between substance and mode to be. Bayle himself is quite insistent that this is the crux of the matter. If there is any mistake in his objections, it lies here. But if he is mistaken, it is Spinoza's fault, not his:

> I took these terms in the sense that all the new philosophers [for example, the Cartesians and Gassendists] understand them
> . . . the general doctrine of the philosophers is that the idea of being contains, immediately under it, two species—substance and accident—and that substance subsists by itself . . . and an accident subsists in some other being . . . They add that "to subsist by itself" signifies only "not being dependent on any subject of inhesion."[13]

Bayle then distinguishes three different views of the nature of accidents held by the philosophers of his time. Some, with the doctrine of transubstantiation in mind, are forced to recognize a "real" distinction between substance and accident, and to admit that an accident can subsist without a subject, though this is contrary to the definition of "accident."

Other philosophers say that, while some accidents are really distinct from their subject, some are not. The accidents which cannot exist apart from their subject they call "modes." And finally,

> Descartes, Gassendi, and in general, all those who have abandoned scholastic philosophy, have denied that an accident is separable from its subject in such a way that it could subsist after separation, and have ascribed to all accidents the nature of those that are called "modes" and have employed the term "mode" . . . rather than that of "accident."

Since Spinoza was "a great Cartesian" it seems only reasonable to suppose that he used these terms in the same way the rest of the new philosophers did, that his modes depend on substance "as on a subject of inhesion." Indeed, Bayle is right, it does seem reasonable—particularly on a superficial comparison of Spinoza's definitions with those in Descartes.

Nevertheless, I am persuaded that this view, for all its initial plausibility, is a mistake. Since Bayle rests his case so heavily on Spinoza's Cartesianism, I shall try to show that he is mistaken by examining some of the differences between Spinoza's philosophical terminology and Descartes'.

We may begin by calling attention to the difficulties that Spinoza's definitions of "substance" and "mode" caused one of his most acute contemporaries. Leibniz received a copy of Spinoza's *Opera Posthuma* shortly after publication, and the reading notes he made on the *Ethics* are very instructive. He complains first that the definition of "substance" is obscure (Gerhardt, I: 139). "For what is it to exist *in se?*" A good question, indeed.

Then he wonders about the second defining phrase. Does Spinoza mean that "substance is what exists in itself *and also* what is conceived through itself? Or does he mean that substance is that in which *both* occur together?" If Spinoza means the latter—as he certainly does—then

"It will be necessary for him to prove that what has the one also has
the other, since, on the contrary, it seems rather that there are some
things which are in themselves, though they are not conceived through
themselves. *And so men commonly conceive of substance.*" Thus we
have an added feature in Spinoza's definition of substance which makes
it puzzling to someone who is thinking in Cartesian terms. For Descartes,
though substance is supposed to exist in itself, it is conceived through
another. The existence of substance, which we do not know immediately,
is inferred from the existence of its attribute, which we do know immediately. Descartes' doctrine is that we cannot know the existence of substance merely from its being a thing that needs only itself in order to
exist. Thus Spinoza very probably has Descartes in mind when he writes
that those who confuse substances and modifications will find the demonstration that it pertains to the nature of substance to exist (*E* I P7)
hard to follow:

> But if men were to consider the nature of substance, they would
> not entertain the slightest doubts about the truth of P7; indeed
> this proposition would be numbered among the common notions.
> For they would understand by substance what is in itself and is
> conceived through itself, that is, *that whose knowledge does not
> require the knowledge of any other thing.*[14]

Spinoza has added a clause to his definition of "substance" that dis-
qualifies most of the things Descartes would call substances from being
so classified. An entity whose existence must be inferred from the existence of something else, whose knowledge requires the knowledge of
another thing, such as an attribute, would not be a substance in Spinoza's
sense of the term.

This is not, I think, a mere exclusion by definition. Spinoza's view
is that anything which really exists in itself must be conceived through
itself. He does not, as Leibniz would have him do, undertake to prove
this. But he could, by arguing: (1) that knowledge of an effect depends

on and involves knowledge of its cause ($E$ IA4); (2) that what exists
in itself is not the effect of any external cause;[15] (3) that, therefore,
knowledge of what exists in itself does not depend on or involve knowledge of anything else; and (4) since what is not conceived through
anything else must be conceived through itself ($E$ IA2), what exists
in itself must also be conceived through itself.[16] Thus the notion of
something existing in itself, but conceived through something else—the
usual, Cartesian notion of substance—is self-contradictory.

For his part, Leibniz does not merely find the notion that substance
must be conceived through itself as well as exist in itself an unconven-
tional one. He argues that it involves an inconsistency with the definition
of "attribute." For Spinoza says in that definition

> that an attribute is perceived by the intellect as constituting the
> essence of substance. Therefore, the concept of the attribute is
> necessary to form the concept of substance. If you say that an
> attribute is not a thing and that you really require only that a
> substance does not need the concept of any other thing, I answer
> that you must explain what may be called a thing, so that we
> may understand the definition and understand in what way an
> attribute is not a thing.

The objection Leibniz makes here is natural enough, from a Cartesian
standpoint, but the hypothetical reply he is led to put in Spinoza's mouth
is wrongheaded. It is not that an attribute is not a thing, but that
it is not *another* thing. Spinoza, unlike Descartes, does identify substance
with its attribute, or rather, with the totality of its attributes.

This point is not immediately obvious from Spinoza's definition of
"attribute," but it is suggested by his definition of "God" as a "substance
consisting of infinite attributes" and is confirmed as the *Ethics*
progresses:

> There is nothing outside the intellect by which several things
> can be distinguished from one another, except substances, or

what is the same thing (D4), their attributes, and their affections.
(*E* Ip4D)
 God is eternal, or all of his attributes are eternal. (*E* Ip19)
 God is immutable, or all of his attributes are immutable.
(*E* Ip20c)

The *Correspondence* is decisive on this point. There we find that Spinoza had originally defined "attribute" in much the same way he defined "substance."

> By attribute I understand whatever is conceived through itself and in itself, so that the conception of it does not involve the conception of another thing. (*Ep.* 2, IV:7)

Even after he had changed the definition of "attribute" to what it is in the *Ethics,* he regarded these terms as two names for the same thing:

> By substance I understand what is in itself and is conceived through itself, that is, that whose concept does not involve the concept of another thing. I understand the same by attribute, except that it is called attribute with respect to the intellect, which attributes such and such a nature to substance. (*Ep.* 9, IV:46)

As an example of how one and the same thing can be called by two names, he offers the third patriarch, who was called both Israel and Jacob. So substance is not, as with Descartes, a distinct entity. It is the attributes themselves.

Because Spinoza does not distinguish attribute from substance, he will allow that his attributes possess the defining characteristics of substance. That "every attribute . . . must be conceived through itself" is explicitly a theorem of Spinoza's system (*E* Ip10). And it is not difficult to construct a proof that what is conceived through itself must exist in itself. For if it existed in something else, knowledge of it would depend on knowledge of that in which it existed (by *E* I A4), and it would not be conceived through itself.[17] Leibniz, therefore, is wrong when he says that modes differ from attributes in that "an attribute exists . . . in a substance but is conceived through itself," whereas modes exist in *and* are conceived through substance. In Spinoza's scheme of things, each attribute exists in itself and is conceived through itself.

This example alone is enough to show that Spinoza's use of these terms is highly idiosyncratic. But further differences appear when we examine his notion of a mode. Spinoza's modes are, prima facie, of the wrong logical type to be related to substance in the same way Descartes' modes are related to substance, for they are particular things (*E* I P25C), not qualities. And it is difficult to know what it would mean to say that particular things inhere in substance. When qualities are said to inhere in substance, this may be viewed as a way of saying that they are predicated of it. What it would mean to say that one thing is predicated of another is a mystery that needs solving.

No doubt we can *give* a sense to the statement that one thing is predicated of another. Bayle, in effect, does this by interpreting Spinoza's doctrine that every finite thing is a mode of God to mean that every property of every finite thing is predicable of God. But once we see that something of this sort must be done, the assimilation of Spinoza to Descartes loses a good deal of its initial plausibility.

These two features of Spinoza's philosophical terminology—that his modes are particular things and that his substance is not distinguished from its attributes—may help to explain the fact, pointed out by H. A. Wolfson, that the term "subject," which figures so prominently in traditional definitions of substance is absent from Spinoza's. Neither his modes nor his attributes can exist in substance as in a subject, they do not inhere in substance. For the attributes do not exist in anything other than themselves, and the modes are themselves the sort of thing that would properly be the subject of predication. It may be too much to say, as Wolfson does, that the term "subject" has no meaning at all for Spinoza (I, 72). He does, after all, use the notion of existence in a subject on occasion (*E* IIIp5). But we can accurately say that the term would have been of no use to him in explaining the relationship of either attributes or modes to substance.

When Spinoza does undertake to characterize the relation between modes and substance—beyond saying that they exist in it and are conceived through it—the terms he uses are quite different. He says that God is the cause of the things that are in him (*E* Ip18d), that he has produced them (*E* Ip24), that he has determined them (*E* Ip26), or that they follow from him (*E* Ip28d). And since he identifies substance and attribute, he is just as likely to say that the modes are determined by, or produced by, or follow from an attribute of God, or the absolute nature of an attribute of God (*E* Ip21–23; *E* Ip28d). This terminology may be vague and confusing. Indeed, its clarification will take all of the next chapter. But it does not in the least suggest inherence in a subject. What it does suggest is merely some kind of causal dependence.

It may be, of course, that Bayle himself did not take this interpretation seriously. Bayle's intentions are a paradigm of obscurity. According to one very popular view, his professed fideism is merely a way of concealing his true purpose, which is to destroy orthodoxy by showing its absurdity. Because he claims to believe what is absurd in spite of its absurdity, he is protected from those in authority. But he gets his real message across to the free spirits who know how to read him.

So, it might be argued, Bayle's real target is not the alleged atheism of Spinoza, but the doctrines of transubstantiation and the Trinity. These, he suggests, are quite similar to his version of Spinozism and appear "contrary to the most distinct notions of our minds" in just the same way. Bayle is very careful to point out where the flaw in his interpretation of Spinoza must lie, if there is any. He acknowledges that the usual reading of Spinoza is different on this point. And he supports his own treatment of Spinoza with arguments that are sometimes very peculiar.[18]

Moreover, the charge that Spinoza's system is false because it is contrary to the most distinct notions of our minds sounds very odd, coming from a philosopher whose official position is that some propositions which seem self-evidently true are nonetheless known to be false.[19] And Bayle does put into Spinoza's mouth some very cogent criticisms of orthodox doctrine, which Bayle counters quite weakly.[20]

All of this does seem rather suspicious. For my purposes, however, it does not really matter. I am concerned not with Bayle's sincerity, but with his accuracy and cogency. If he did not really accept this interpretation himself, then I suppose that is all the more reason why we should not. But Bayle's line still has enough followers to deserve critical examination.

The views of H. H. Joachim are in many ways remarkably like Bayle's, although they seem to have been arrived at independently. Joachim begins his treatment of the definitions of substance and mode with the statement that, for Spinoza,

> The subject matter of philosophy, the Real, falls apart into two great divisions:—that which is in itself and that which is in something else. "That which is in itself," i.e., that the reality of which is self-dependent, is what Spinoza calls "substance"; "that whose reality is dependent" is called a "mode" or state of substance. We begin, therefore, with the antithesis of Substance and its states or modifications—a more precise formulation of the popular antithesis of thing and properties, the metaphysical . . . correlate of the logical antithesis of subject and predicate. (*Study*, pp. 14–15)

Let me say immediately that most of what Joachim says in this passage seems to be perfectly correct. He is quite right, I think, to maintain that the distinction between substance and mode is a distinction between independent (or self-dependent) and dependent beings. What I balk at is the identification of this distinction with the distinction between things and properties, or subjects and predicates. For a philosopher like Descartes, or Locke, or Arnauld, these distinctions are run together, and in this Descartes and Locke and Arnauld represent a tradition going back ultimately to Aristotle. But it is one of Spinoza's principal novelties that he breaks with this long tradition.

I have already indicated my main reasons for this contention, and there is no need to repeat them here. What I wish to do now is to consider some of the conclusions Joachim comes to concerning the status of finite modes in Spinoza's system as a result of his interpretation of the definitions of substance and mode.

Roughly, his position is this: particular things may be viewed in either one of two ways—as parts of *natura naturata* or as parts of the common order of nature. In so far as they are viewed as parts of *natura naturata,* they are seen in the context of a modal system which expresses God's nature and are seen to be timelessly and necessarily actual. And this is the way they really are. But so viewed, their particularity vanishes. They are completely real, but not individually distinct. Individuality can properly be attributed only to God.

On the other hand, in so far as particular things are viewed as part of the common order of nature, they are seen in abstraction from the modal system on which they depend and are considered to be individually distinct but finite, transitory, and not completely real. This is the world of presentation, the phenomenal world, in which things occur at a particular time and place, interact with one another, result from infinitely long chains of causes, initiate infinitely long chains of effects, change, come into being, and pass away. These occurrences are unintelligible and fortuitous, although ascribed to necessary and universal laws. And this world is never more than an illusion.

Thus, Spinoza's metaphysic turns out to be monistic in a very strict Eleatic sense. Spinoza's substance, Joachim says, "is one (not as a unity of diverse but related elements, but) as a unity which has overcome and taken into itself the distinctness of its diverse elements, and this absorption is so complete that in it there remain no 'elements,' no distinctness, no articulation" (p. 108). For all things are merely states of the one substance, God. It is only by an abstraction that they can be treated as independent things and made the subjects of judgments. Somehow, in some sense, it is God who is the subject (p. 127).

Such, in brief, is the picture Joachim gives us of this aspect of Spinoza's metaphysics. It is a difficult picture to get clear in one's mind, and no doubt in abstracting from the rich diversity of Joachim's language, I have to some extent misrepresented him. But there is no alternative, short of a much longer discussion than there is time or space for.

Joachim, like Bayle, deduces a number of highly paradoxical consequences from his interpretation of Spinoza's definitions of substance and mode. Unlike Bayle, however, he does not rest the attribution of these paradoxes to Spinoza solely on that interpretation. A full discussion of his version of Spinoza's metaphysics would require lengthy excursions into Spinoza's theory of mind, his epistemology, and the murky regions of the fifth part of the *Ethics*. As far as possible, I shall try to avoid such excursions, with the result that this discussion will not be a full one. But I do wish to say something, briefly, about two points in Joachim's interpretation.

The first is the denial of real individuality to particular things. In part, this is simply a deduction from his interpretation of the definitions of substance and mode. If the distinction between substance and mode is merely a more precise formulation of the distinction between things and properties, and if there is only one substance, then there is really only one thing. If there appear to be many things, this must be an illusion.

In part, however, the denial of individuality to particular things rests on the fact that, for Spinoza, each particular thing is enmeshed in a network of causal relations:

> A single "extended" thing—a particular body, e.g.,—is finite and dependent; a fragment torn from its context, in which alone it has being and significance. Neither in its existence, nor in its nature has it any independence. It owes its existence to an indefinite chain of causes, each of which is itself a finite body and the effect of

> a finite body; it owes its nature to its place in the whole system
> of bodies which together constitute the corporeal universe. Any
> attempt to explain it—to understand its essential nature—would
> carry you outside "it," or would force you to regard "it" as having
> no essential nature or individuality; for "it" is through and through
> constituted by its relations, and if you include them in "its" nature,
> "it" will have become merged in the whole attribute of extension.
> (p. 23)

This is the familiar "flower-in-the-crannied-wall" motif. And no doubt
a good part of what Joachim says here is correct. Spinoza does, of
course, hold that finite bodies depend for their existence on other finite
bodies (*E* Ip28). I think I should have said that they depend for their
nature, not on their "place in the whole system of bodies," but on the
attributes and the infinite modes. But that is a difficult point, and in
any case the natures of particular things do depend on something outside
those things. And since knowledge of an effect depends on and involves
knowledge of its cause, understanding the essential nature of a body
would require going outside it.

However, Spinoza never infers from these facts that bodies have no
essential nature or individuality. He denies explicitly that their essential
nature is constituted by their relations.[21] And in the later parts of the
*Ethics* he seems to identify the essence of particular things with the
force by which they persevere in existence (*E* IIp45s; *E* IIIp6, 7).
Indeed, this notion is so important for Spinoza's ethical theory that
it is difficult to see how he could deny that things have an essential
nature.[22]

Moreover, the view that the individuality of particular things is swal-
lowed up in that of the whole whose parts they are seems quite contrary
to the discussion that follows *E* IIp13. There Spinoza is concerned to
show how the whole of nature can be conceived as one individual,
"whose parts, that is, all bodies, differ in infinite ways without any
change in the whole individual" (*E* IIL7s). He begins by considering

the simplest bodies, which are distinguished from one another by motion and rest or speed and slowness. This he supposes to be self-evident. He then posits that a composite body will constitute one body or individual if its parts communicate their motion to one another in a certain fixed proportion. So long as the parts preserve toward one another the same kind of motion and rest, the individual will retain the same nature—even if the parts are replaced by others. Composite bodies may be of varying orders of complexity; some are composed only of simple bodies, others are composed of parts which are themselves composite. But the principle in virtue of which a composite is regarded as one individual is the same, regardless of its complexity. And it is in this way that the whole of nature can be conceived as one individual.

Now the interesting thing about this discussion is that Spinoza seems to regard the individuality of these simplest bodies as something that is immediately intelligible, whereas he regards the individuality of the whole of nature as something requiring a long and elaborate explanation. But on Joachim's version of Spinoza, it is the other way around.[23] Only the whole of nature is truly an individual. The individuality of finite "things" is an illusion of the finite intellect—an illusion which is very difficult to understand because this finite intellect is itself supposed to be an illusion.

The discussion which follows *E* IIP13 is, of course, nothing but an elaboration of *E* IID7: "By singular things I understand things which are finite and have a determinate existence; and if several individuals [*NS*: or singular things] so concur in one action that they are all simultaneously the cause of one effect, I consider them all, *so far* [my italics], as one individual thing." The qualification "so far" should be enough by itself to assure us that Spinoza does not think that particular things lose their individuality by being considered as parts of a composite individual.

The second matter which requires comment is the attribution to Spinoza of illusionism. Joachim is not clear how far he wants to go in this. In one place, he says that "the world of presentation—the world of things in time and place . . . is not, it seems, ever more than a mere illusion" (pp. 112–113). But earlier he says that "this world of isolated and perishable things, with its apparently arbitrary sequences . . . this world of the unscientific experience is largely illusory . . . But it is not through and through illusion: or, if it is, there must at least be a real basis of the illusion" (pp. 79–80). Thus, the phenomenal world may, perhaps, be something more than an illusion. The reason for this hesitation is that Joachim's Spinoza must explain the illusion as due to the defects of the finite human intellect, thereby implicitly attributing some reality to finite things. Spinoza, Joachim says, is "far too ready to dismiss things as 'mere illusions' " (p. 114), for he needs them to explain the fact of the illusion.

In part, again, I think this is a deduction from Joachim's interpretation of the definitions of substance and mode. For him, Spinoza's substance is a unity in which there are no real distinctions. The phenomenal world is a plurality of distinct entities, so the phenomenal world must be an illusion. But Joachim also apppeals to passages where Spinoza says such things as: "The human mind, whenever it perceives things from the common order of nature, has adequate knowledge neither of itself, nor of its own body, nor of external bodies, but only a confused and mutilated knowledge" (*E* IIP29c). So to evaluate Joachim's interpretation, we need to understand the meaning of phrases like "perception of things from the common order of nature" and "adequate knowledge." For Spinoza never *says* that the world of the finite is an illusion, and we must know whether what he does say entails that it is an illusion, a deceptive appearance of a reality which is in fact quite different from what it seems to be.

In the scholium to the corollary quoted above, Spinoza explains what he intends by the phrase "perception from the common order of nature" in the following way:

> I say expressly that the mind has adequate knowledge neither of
> itself, nor of its body, nor of external bodies, but only a confused and

> mutilated knowledge, whenever it perceives things from the com-
> mon order of nature, that is, whenever it is determined to con-
> templating this or that externally, from what is indeed a chance
> meeting with things—and not when it is determined to understand-
> ing their agreements, differences and oppositions internally, from
> the fact that it contemplates several things at once. For whenever
> it is ordered internally, in this or some other way, then it contem-
> plates things clearly and distinctly.

This explanation is not as helpful as we might wish, but it is at least
clear that "perception from the common order of nature" is another
name for what is elsewhere called "knowledge of the first kind, or opinion, or imagination" (*E* IIp40s2; *TdIE,* 19, II: 10). Of this, Spinoza
distinguishes two subclasses: knowledge from report or signs, such as
the knowledge I have of my birthday or my parentage, and knowledge
from vagrant experience (*experientia vaga*), such as my knowledge
that I, being a man like other men, will some day die or that water
extinguishes fire. These are all things I know because I happen to have
been so placed in the world that I have had experiences of one kind
and not those of a contrary kind. All the water I have seen has, when
put to the test, extinguished fire. Thus, I am determined to these perceptions externally and fortuitously. For I have experienced only a very
small part of what might have been experienced, and what I have seen
may be misleading. My ideas are very inadequate, they do not have
all the properties or internal marks of a true idea (*E* IID4), they are
not clear and distinct.

  On the other hand, when my perceptions are determined internally,
then my knowledge is either of the second kind, reason, which perceives
the thing in question through having the common notions and adequate
ideas of the properties of things, or of the third kind, intuition, which
proceeds from an adequate idea of the essence of a divine attribute
to an adequate knowledge of the essences of things. Spinoza commonly
illustrates the differences between these different kinds of knowledge

by appealing to a mathematical example. Suppose we are given three numbers, $a$, $b$, and $c$, and told to find a fourth which bears the same ratio to $c$ as $b$ does to $a$. We may have been taught in school to multiply $b$ and $c$, dividing their product by $a$ to find the correct answer. This would be knowledge from report, one form of opinion. Or we may discover this rule for ourselves by experimenting with cases where the answer is obvious and generalizing from them. This inductive procedure would yield knowledge from vagrant experience, another form of opinion. But if we have studied Euclid, we will know that this is the procedure to follow because we understand the common property of proportionals. This would be knowledge of the second kind, reason. And if the numbers are very simple ones, we may see at a glance what the ratio is between $a$ and $b$ and infer from this the correct answer. This would be intuition, or knowledge of the third kind.

Now there is much that is difficult in this classification of the kinds of knowledge. But this much can be said. Spinoza is distinguishing between the various ways in which we may attain knowledge. And the principal thing is that some of them (reason, intuition) give adequate ideas, which bear all the internal marks of truth, and therefore are certainly true, whereas the others (report, vagrant experience) give inadequate ideas, which do not bear all the internal marks of truth, are not clear and distinct, and therefore are not known with certainty to be true.

But it does not follow that perceptions stemming from these latter sources are false. After all, Spinoza's example indicates that even the eternal truths of mathematics may be, and perhaps in most cases are, known through one of these defective modes of cognition. So a perception arising from the common order of nature is merely uncertain and need not misrepresent reality. No doubt such perceptions often do, and according to Spinoza knowledge of the first kind is the only cause of falsity ($E$ IIp41). But perceptions from the common order of nature are not—as Joachim's talk of illusions unfortunately suggests—invariably false. And Spinoza evidently reposed enough faith in them to be able

to assert, as a corollary to *E* IIP13, that the human body does exist
*as we perceive it,* in spite of the fact that our perception of it from
the common order of nature is inadequate.[24] So the talk of inadequate
knowledge gives us no warrant at all for dismissing the phenomenal
world as a mere illusion. And an interpretation of Spinoza's definitions
of substance and mode which is reduced to such desperate expedients
needs more supporting evidence than it has ever been given.

## The Wolfson Interpretation

In 1934, there appeared on the scene an alternative interpretation
of Spinoza's definitions, put forward with overwhelming erudition by
H. A. Wolfson. Though diametrically opposed to the line of interpretation followed by Bayle and Joachim, it too has a very high degree of
initial plausibility and has achieved sufficiently wide acceptance that
it is already beginning to appear in textbooks on the history of philosophy.[25] Wolfson takes us on an exciting philosophical journey, beyond
Descartes and the rest of Spinoza's contemporaries, back through the
medievals to Aristotle, in an attempt to reconstruct the *Ethica More
Scholastico Rabbinicoque Demonstrata* which must have preceded, in
Spinoza's mind, the *Ethica Ordine Geometrico Demonstrata* which was
left us at Spinoza's death. It is the evidence for this reconstruction that
we must now examine.

On this interpretation, the term "substance" denotes the *summum
genus,* Substance; the term "mode" denotes individuals, or individual
essences; and the relation of mode to substance is a relation of individual
or species to genus. When Spinoza says that the modes *exist in* substance,
he is using this phrase in the same sense Aristotle uses when he says
that "man is 'in' animal, and generally species 'in' genus" (*Physics,*
210a, 18). But Substance, since it is the *summum genus,* does not exist
in anything else in that sense, it is not a species of any genus, and
so it must be said to exist in itself.

This view has its own, very considerable historical precedent and,
it would seem, great explanatory power. Consider, for example, the

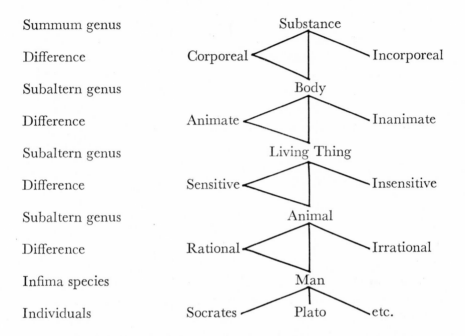

| Summum genus | Substance | |
| Difference | Corporeal | Incorporeal |
| Subaltern genus | Body | |
| Difference | Animate | Inanimate |
| Subaltern genus | Living Thing | |
| Difference | Sensitive | Insensitive |
| Subaltern genus | Animal | |
| Difference | Rational | Irrational |
| Infima species | Man | |
| Individuals | Socrates    Plato | etc. |

famous tree of Porphyry above. "Substance" here appears as the name of the genus under which all other genera are subsumed. It is thus not a species of any other genus, and in that sense exists in itself. But the essences of all individuals, their *infimae species,* ultimately exist in substance as a species in its genus, and in that sense exist in another.

Moreover, this interpretation allows Wolfson to give a very likely-looking explanation of that feature of Spinoza's definitions of substance and mode which so puzzled Leibniz. Spinoza says that substance is what exists in itself *and is conceived through itself* and that mode is what exists in another, *through which it is conceived.* What do these additional phrases mean and how can they be accounted for? Wolfson is ready with the answer. In Aristotelian logic, we are told, genera and species

perform certain functions in the formation of concepts. They are the elements, or rather the causes, in the terms of which the individual essence, the "what" of it, can be conceived. They form its definition.

> Man is thus conceived through his genus "animal" and his species
> [difference?] "rational," and he is thus also defined by the combina-
> tion of these two terms. And so everything that is in something
> else, as an individual in its genus, may be thus said to be conceived
> by that something else. (I, 76)

Substance, on the other hand, as it is not a species of any genus, is
not conceived through anything else. Hence, by *E* Ia2, it must be conceived through itself. Wolfson, however, regards the phrase "conceived
through itself" as having a purely negative import, so that the axiom
"Whatever is not conceived through something else must be conceived
through itself" is a disguised tautology, and the implication of saying
that substance is conceived through itself is that "Spinoza's substance
is inconceivable, and its essence undefinable, and hence, unknowable."
And this agrees with the medieval doctrine according to which that
unique substance, God, is undefinable and in his essence unknowable.

Wolfson's interpretation has other fruitful consequences. For instance,
it provides an apparent explanation of Spinoza's view that substance
is prior in nature to its modes (*E* Ip1), since Wolfson can point to
the Aristotelian principle that the genus is prior to the individual
(*Topics*, 141a, 26ff). Again, when Spinoza says that God is the immanent cause of all things (*E* Ip18), Wolfson explains this by adducing
Maimonidean and Aristotelian texts according to which the genus is
the internal cause of the species or individual essence (I, 319–324).

And so it goes. Wolfson begins his work by claiming that if we had
all the philosophical literature available to Spinoza, we could reconstruct
nearly the whole of the *Ethics* just by making appropriate selections
and arrangements of the doctrines of his predecessors. This is an extreme
thesis—one which Wolfson is forced, later, to qualify in curious ways,[26]
and one which makes Spinoza's originality quite problematic. But
Wolfson defends it very persuasively.

Nevertheless, I shall contend that this interpretation of the definitions
is fundamentally incoherent and that some, at least, of the consequences

Wolfson draws from his interpretation are in clear conflict with Spinoza's explicit doctrine.

First, let us reflect that like most of the philosophers of his time, but unlike most of the medievals, Spinoza has, in general, little use for arguments from authority. The knowledge we have of things from report only is hardly worthy of the name knowledge. Indeed, in the *Short Treatise* (*KV* II, i, I:54) Spinoza says that the man who applies the rule of three to find the fourth proportional merely because this is what he has been told to do has no more knowledge of the rule than a blind man has of color. And, in particular, he has little use for the authority of Aristotle. Writing to Hugo Boxel, who had tried to persuade him of the existence of ghosts, he says that

> To me the authority of Plato, Aristotle, and Socrates is not worth much. Had you cited Epicurus, Democritus, Lucretius, or any of the atomists and defenders of atoms, I would have been astonished. But it is no cause for wonder that those who invented occult qualities, intentional species, substantial forms, and a thousand other trifles, devised specters and ghosts and trusted old women in order to weaken the authority of Democritus. They were so envious of his good reputation that they burned all his books, which he had published with great praise. If you are disposed to put faith in them, what reason have you for denying the miracles of the Holy Virgin and all the Saints? These have been described by so many illustrious philosophers, theologians, and historians, that I could produce a hundred of them against hardly one of the other. (*Ep.* 56, IV:261–262)

This does not sound much like a man whose work would first have been composed *more scholastico rabbinicoque*.

Again, consider the identification of Spinoza's one substance with the *summum genus* of traditional philosophy. This is to say, in effect, that the only thing which satisfies the definition of "substance" is the

genus Substance itself. To be a substance, for Wolfson's Spinoza, is
to be not-in-anything-as-a-species-is-in-its-genus. The genus Substance
is not-in-anything-as-a-species-is-in-its-genus, for it is the *summum
genus.* The genus Substance is, therefore, a substance, a member of
the genus Substance. And since, for anybody's Spinoza, there is only
one thing that satisfies the definition of substance, the genus Substance
must be the only thing that is not-in-anything-as-a-species-is-in-its-genus.
Everything else must be a species of some genus, including individuals.

Now this, if you stop to think about it, is a very strange doctrine
indeed. First of all, it requires us to treat a class, the genus Substance,
as a member of itself. And many logicians nowadays, with Russell's
paradoxes in mind, would reject the notion of a class being a member
of itself as unintelligible. Not every logician today would reject it, and
even if every logician did, this fact by itself would do nothing to show
what Spinoza's views are. But anyone who feels uncomfortable with
classes that are members of themselves will naturally suspect that an
interpretation which requires them may run into other difficulties as
well.

And so it does. Consider the identification of Spinoza's modes with
"individuals" or "individual essences." It may have been noticed that
Wolfson, with a nice disregard for logical proprieties, uses these two
notions interchangeably. But surely they cannot be so used.[27] If the
modes are individuals, then they cannot be said to exist in Substance
as a species exists in its genus. We must say that they exist in Substance
as an individual in its genus. And Wolfson does say this in various
places. But this cannot be a correct account of Spinoza's philosophy.
For if the modes exist in Substance as individuals exist in a genus,
then the modes are, in plain language, substances. For a genus must
always be predicable of the individuals that exist in it.

So the modes must be individual essences and their relation to Substance must be that of species to genus, in spite of the fact that Spinoza
calls them individual things. It is something of a mystery what the status
of individual things would be on this interpretation. They are evidently

not modes, they cannot be substances, and these are presumably the only two categories available. Perhaps, appearances to the contrary, there are no individual things, only genera and species, though this would hardly seem Aristotelian, much less Spinozistic.

These are, of course, not decisive objections. They raise questions about the coherence of Wolfson's interpretation or about its compatibility with Spinoza's presumed spirit and tendencies, but do not show it to be wrong. There are, however, other objections, which are of a textual nature and are, it seems to me, decisive.

In the first place, it is not at all clear that Spinoza would regard the genus Substance as the *summum genus*. Bayle, it will be recalled, said that the general doctrine of the philosophers of his time was that Being is the *summum genus,* and that Substance is a species of the genus Being. There may be good reason for denying this, on the traditional ground that "Being" is not predicated univocally of the categories, but there are very strong indications that this was also Spinoza's view. In his *Metaphysical Thoughts,* he begins by defining "Being," and goes on to remark that from his definition, it is easily seen that: "Being is to be divided into being which exists necessarily, or whose essence involves existence, and into being whose essence involves only possible existence" (*CM* I, i, I:236). This last category, he says, is divided into substance and modes. Here he is in part expounding the views of Descartes. If he were speaking for himself, he would make the division between substance and mode correspond to that between necessary and contingent being; it would not be a subdivision of contingent being. But there is every reason to suppose that he would regard the genus Substance as a subaltern genus of the genus Being. In the *Ethics* he treats Being explicitly as the *summum genus:* "We are accustomed to refer all individuals in nature to one genus which is called the most general, that is, to the notion of Being, which embraces absolutely all the individuals in nature" (*E* IV pref., II:207). In the traditional Aristotelian philosophy, it could be said of Substance that it embraces all individuals in nature because entities in the other categories are not individuals but qualities, relations, and so forth. But in Spinoza's philosophy, this could not be said, since the category of mode includes individuals. Nor would the traditional ground for denying that Being is the *summum genus* hold, for there is a definition of "being" which can be predicated univocally of both substances and modes.

But quite apart from the question whether Spinoza would regard Substance as the *summum genus,* it seems highly unlikely that he would be willing to treat any genus as the cause of all things. In the *Treatise on the Correction of the Intellect,* he writes that

> We should inquire whether there is any being, and if so, what sort of being there is, which is the cause of all things. In this way the being's subjective essence [*essentia objectiva,* used in the Cartesian sense, as a representation in the intellect of an external reality] will be the cause of all our ideas, and our mind, as we have said, will reflect Nature as far as possible. For the mind will have subjectively Nature's essence and order and union. From this we can see that, above all, it is necessary for us always to deduce all our ideas from physical things, that is, from real entities, proceeding, as far as possible, according to the series of causes, from one real entity to another, so that we do not pass over to abstractions and universals, lest we either infer something real from them, or infer them from something real. Both inferences break the true progress of the intellect. (*TdIE,* 99, II:36)

From this it seems clear enough that universals and abstractions, under which heading genera and species fall, are not regarded by Spinoza as real beings, and hence not possible candidates for the cause of all things, substance.[28]

These facts—that Spinoza did not regard Substance as the *summum genus* and that he denied the reality and causal efficacy of universals— weigh very heavily against Wolfson's contention that the modes exist in substance "as a species in its genus," and also against his related interpretation of the doctrine that God is the immanent cause of all things.

There is a similar objection to his explanation of the doctrine that the modes are conceived through substance in terms of the Aristotelian view that individual essences are conceived through the genera and species which form their definitions. For in rejecting the notion of universals as causes, Spinoza also rejects the theory of definition associated with it. This may be seen in the *Short Treatise,* where he takes up the "specious arguments" by which traditional philosophers "seek to excuse their lack of knowledge of God" (*KV* I, vii, I:46). One of these arguments is that God, because he is not a species of any genus, cannot be properly defined, for a correct definition must be by genus and difference.

Spinoza replies that "although all logicians admit this, I do not know where they get it from." For if it is true, we can have no knowledge at all. Knowing a thing perfectly, on the traditional view, involves knowing it through a definition by genus and difference. From this it follows that we cannot know perfectly the *summum genus* because it has no genus above it and cannot be given a definition by genus and difference. But on this traditional view, the *summum genus* is supposed to be the cause of our knowledge of all other things. If it is not known, then none of the things that are explained by that genus can be understood or known—that is, nothing at all can be known. Hence, Spinoza proposes a new theory of definition, "following our division of nature," according to which things will not be defined by genus and difference.

Definitions, he says, must be of two kinds. Those of things which subsist through themselves, the attributes, "need no genus, or anything, through which they might be better understood or explained." Those of things which do not exist through themselves, the modes, require a reference to their attribute, "through which, *as their genus,* they must be understood." Spinoza does not elaborate further on this new theory of definition in the *Short Treatise.*

In the *Treatise on the Correction of the Intellect* (*TdIE,* 96–97, II:35–36), however, he gives a fuller account. There he makes it clear that the phrase "as their genus" must not be pressed too far. The attributes are not related to modes as genus to individual. The phrase "as their genus" indicates a comparison only. For the first rule for the definition of created things is that the definition must mention their proximate causes. And Spinoza later explains that the proximate causes are his fixed and eternal things, which, *"though they are singulars,* on account of their presence everywhere and their most extensive power, will be to us like universals, or genera of the definitions of singular mutable things" (*TdIE,* 101, II:37).

It is clear, I think, that Spinoza could make precisely the same objection to Wolfson's interpretation of Spinozism that he makes to the traditional philosophers who seek to excuse their ignorance in theology. By identifying God or substance with the *summum genus,* through which all things are supposed to be conceived, and then declaring, as on the traditional theory he must, that Spinoza's substance is inconceivable, Wolfson commits Spinoza to the same absurdity Spinoza is complaining of in the traditional philosophers: nothing is knowable.

And of course, as we might expect from all this, Spinoza's God is not—though Wolfson says he is—inconceivable. His essence is not undefinable and unknowable. For quite apart from the fact that Spinoza gives us a definition of God (*E* ID6), he also proves, as a theorem, that "the human mind possesses an adequate knowledge of the eternal and infinite essence of God" (*E* IIP47). It would be difficult, I suppose, to find so bold a claim in any prior philosophical literature, even if we were to include what was not available to Spinoza. But perhaps that indicates the defects of an excessively historical approach.

## Notes Toward a New Interpretation of Spinoza's Definitions

The moral I am inclined to draw from this discussion is that if we attempt to interpret Spinoza very much along the lines of some one or another of his predecessors, we will be hard put to make sense of his philosophy and are likely to find ourselves attributing to him doctrines that are foreign to his thought. We might say of Spinoza's metaphysics what Artemus Ward is reputed to have said of the early English: "The researches of many eminent antiquarians have already thrown much darkness on the subject; and it is probable, if they continue their labors, that we shall soon know nothing at all about it." This is not to suggest that Spinoza's concept of substance bears no relation at all to traditional concepts of substance. It does. But the precise nature of that relationship needs some examining.

It is often said that Spinoza arrived at the main doctrines of his philosophy by following out the logical consequences of the Cartesian concept of substance. And in a sense, that is certainly true; but only in a sense. The Cartesian distinction between substance and mode, as we have seen, involved two elements: a distinction between independent and dependent being and a distinction between subject and predicate. And these two distinctions were usually thought to coincide: the subjects of predication were thought to be independent entities and the qualities predicated of them were regarded as dependent. If I understand him correctly, Spinoza, in classifying particular things as modes, was intent on emphasizing the fact that the two distinctions do not coincide, that what is the subject of predication is not an independent entity. He did not intend to say that the relation of particular things to God was in any way like the relation of a predicate to its subject.

This does not mean merely that he recognized and insisted upon the Scholastic and Cartesian commonplace that the finite things which are subjects of predication are not strictly substances because of their dependence on God. It means also that he would not accord them even that relative independence which they possess in Descartes. Thus in the preface to his *Principles of Cartesian Philosophy,* when he wishes to give examples of points on which he disagrees with the author whom he is expounding, he mentions the Cartesian view that minds and bodies are substances. And he gives as his reason for disagreement, not the fact that minds and bodies depend on God—his version of the Cartesian definition of substance as what requires only the concurrence of God in order to exist (*PP* IID2, I:181) would preclude that objection—but the fact that they depend on other minds and bodies. The immediate issue is whether the will is distinct from the intellect and free. Spinoza objects that

> in these assertions . . . Descartes only stated and did not prove
> that the human mind is absolute thinking substance. Although our
> Author [the preface was written by Lewis Meyer, at Spinoza's direc-
> tion] admits that there is a thinking substance in nature he denies
> that it constitutes the essence of the human mind. He holds that,
> in the same way extension is determined by no limits, thought is
> determined by no limits. And as the human body is not absolute,
> but only extension determined in a certain way, according to the
> laws of extended nature, by motion and rest, so also the mind,
> or the human soul, is not absolute, but only thought determined
> in a certain way, according to the laws of thinking nature, by ideas.

The distinction between the independent and the dependent does not correspond to the distinction between subject and predicate, even if we qualify the notion of independent existence in the way Descartes does.

Of course, the distinctions could be made to correspond, trivially, by saying what Burgersdijck says: that in speaking of independence in this connection we intend to exclude only that kind of dependence which a predicate has on its subject and not any other kind of dependence. But Spinoza does not choose to do this. He simply defines substance in terms of independent existence, taken in the broadest sense. And he makes the contrast between independent and dependent being, not the contrast between subject and predicate, the fundamental antithesis of his philosophy. Insofar as Spinoza retains the notion of independent existence, his concept of substance is a traditional one. But insofar as he makes no use of notions arising from the logical analysis of propositions, it is radically new. It may be, as Russell once said, that "all sound philosophy should begin with an analysis of propositions." But if that is so, then Spinoza's philosophy is unsound.

One consequence of Spinoza's radicalism in regard to his conception of substance is that certain criticisms that have been directed against him are really irrelevant to his philosophy. To take one instance, A. E. Taylor has argued (*Mind*, 55:103–104 [1946]) that Spinoza assumes, falsely, that every true proposition is one which asserts or denies a predicate of a subject. That this is one of Spinoza's assumptions he thinks is clear from the definitions of substance, attribute, and mode, and from the fact that Spinoza does not recognize any other type of existent. That it is false he thinks is clear from the fact that an assertion of a relation between two terms cannot be reduced to the ascription of a predicate to a subject. But as H. F. Hallett has quite correctly replied (*Mind*, 55:286 [1946]), the fact that relations are not thus reducible is quite beside the point. This kind of objection depends on assimilating Spinoza's use of the terms "substance," "attribute," and "mode" to that of his contemporaries; but Spinoza's use is very different.[29]

Again, Russell has argued that because Spinoza's metaphysic requires the concept of substance, and because that concept is "one which neither science nor philosophy can nowadays accept" (p. 601), the metaphysic must be rejected. Russell does not explain, in the passage where he says this, why science and philosophy can no longer accept the concept of substance; but it is clear from his discussion of Berkeley and Hume that he has in mind the empiricist criticisms of the concept of substance held by such people as Descartes and Locke, criticisms which turn primarily on the notion of substance as an imperceptible substratum.[30] If, as I have argued, Spinoza does not conceive of substance in that way, then his concept of substance is not, on the face of it, open to such criticism.

It may be asked, of course, whether the concept of a being independent of all causes is any more intelligible than the concept of an imperceptible substratum. If it is not, then Spinoza is no better off than if he held views similar to those of Locke and Descartes.

The brief answer to this, I think, is that the concept of an independent being is just as intelligible as the concept of a dependent one. Since we know what it means to say that one thing depends on another, we must know what it means to say that it does *not* depend on another. And the idea of an independent being is simply the idea of a being that does not depend on any other. We may think, on empirical grounds, that there is no such independent being. Everything, as far as our experience goes, is dependent in nature. And presumably if there is no independent being, then the concept of an independent being is a useless one. But to say this is not to say that it is unintelligible.

This answer, however, is not adequate. For one thing, though we may know what *we* mean when we say, in ordinary circumstances, that one thing depends on another, it is not at all clear what it means to say, in Spinoza's system, that one thing depends on another. I have argued that the relation of mode to substance is a relation of causal dependence which is unlike the relation of predicate to subject and unlike the relation of species to genus. But I have not said what this relation is like. To that extent, then, the definitions of "substance" and "mode" have been left very vague.

Again, someone might argue that, by defining substance as what exists in itself and is conceived through itself, Spinoza does not mean to say merely that it is independent of all external causes. He means also that it is the cause of its own existence, or that its essence involves existence ($E$ Id1). It is not, or not merely, the negative notion of independent existence, but also the positive notion of an existence which is logically necessary and consequently self-explanatory. It would be better to speak of a self-dependent or self-sufficient being. For Spinoza, the concept of substance involves the ontological argument and is only as acceptable as that argument.

There is a good deal of force to this objection. However, it is not quite accurate, as I see it, to say that the definition of substance in itself involves the ontological argument. Spinoza is not defining substance as a being whose essence involves existence. He is defining it as a being that has no external cause. To be sure, it follows from this definition that substance is also a being whose essence involves existence; but that is because Spinoza accepts the principle of sufficient reason in a particularly strong form. Every existing thing has a reason or cause for its existence; if that reason or cause is not external to the thing, then it must lie in the nature of the thing itself (*E* Ip1 1D2). Since substance cannot, by definition, have an external cause, it must be its own cause (*E* Ip7D and *E* Ip6CD2). Hence, the objection is not so much to the concept of substance per se as to the strong form in which Spinoza accepts the principle of sufficient reason. This is a small point, but it is just as well to be accurate about such matters. Nevertheless, the fact remains that Spinoza is committed to the ontological argument, and this seems as good a reason for rejecting his metaphysic as any.

It is tempting to try to defend the ontological argument in Spinoza along the following lines. We might argue that in Spinoza the function of the ontological argument is different than in such writers as Anselm and Descartes. Its purpose is not to prove the existence of a being whose existence is questionable, namely, God, but to justify the deification of a being whose existence no one doubts, namely, Nature.[31] If Nature can be said to have some, at least, of the properties traditionally ascribed to God, then the identification of Nature with God has some warrant. And of the properties traditionally ascribed to God, necessary existence is one of the most important. Spinoza's ontological argument is a crucial step in what Frederick Pollock calls his "euthanasia of theology."

We may well wonder whether anything is explained by saying that Nature is its own cause. Contemporary philosophers are likely to contend that this is another case where a philosopher has pushed a legitimate kind of inquiry beyond the limits of its meaningfulness. We can ask of any particular, finite thing: "What is the reason or cause of its existence?" But we cannot ask this of the whole of Nature, of the totality of things. The question does not make sense, for there is nothing that could, logically, count as an answer to it.

This, I supppose, is the probable reaction that science and philosophy would nowadays have to Spinoza's principle that everything which exists must have a cause or reason for its existence. And I suppose that a contemporary defender of Spinoza might reply on his behalf that saying the question does not make sense, cannot logically make sense, when asked of the whole of Nature is not very different from saying that Nature is its own cause. It seems to be just another way of dissolving the sense of the mystical which attaches to the fact that the world is.

This defense is tempting, perhaps, but will it do justice to Spinoza? I am not sure. What troubles me is the assumption that what is the cause of its own existence, for Spinoza, is the whole of Nature, that the term "substance," while it connotes independent existence, denotes the totality of things. This is, of course, an assumption that is very often made.[32] And there is some (though surprisingly little) textual support for it. For example, in the *Treatise on the Correction of the Intellect* Spinoza writes that

> Since the origin of nature, as we shall see afterwards, can be conceived neither abstractly nor universally, cannot extend more widely in the understanding than it does in fact, and has no similarity to mutable things, no confusion ought to be feared concerning its idea, provided that we have the standard of truth already mentioned; for this is, in fact, a being unique and infinite, that is, it is all being, beyond which there is no being. (*TdIE*, 76, II:29)

This seems definite enough. But in the same passage just one paragraph earlier, Spinoza refers to the "source and origin of Nature" (*fons et origo Naturae*) as the "primary elements of the whole of nature" (*prima elementa totius Naturae*), which certainly makes the origin of nature appear to be something less than the totality of things. And in the *Short Treatise* (*KV* I, viii, I:47), Spinoza speaks of *dividing* the whole of Nature into *Natura Naturans* (a being conceived clearly and distinctly through itself, without the need of anything else, that is, all the attributes of God, that is, substance or God) and *Natura Naturata* (the modes of substance).

The weight of these passages seems to be in favor of saying that "substance" denotes, not the whole of Nature, but only its active part, its primary elements.[33] And if that is correct, then before we can evaluate the ontological argument, or the concept of substance, or any other aspect of Spinoza's metaphysics, we must ask what in Nature might answer to this description. This is a serious gap in our interpretation of Spinoza.

Another gap occurs in connection with Spinoza's modes. Here the denotation of the term is, in part at least, fairly clear. "Mode" denotes, among other things, particular finite things, individual minds and bodies, for example. But it also denotes certain things such as motion and rest, which Spinoza describes as an infinite and eternal mode of the attribute of extension. And these infinite modes are rather mysterious entities.

Moreover, as noted above, the connotation of the term "mode" has been left very vague, in that the nature of its dependence on substance has been specified only negatively, by saying that it is not the dependence of a predicate on its subject, and not the dependence of a species on its genus. Something more definite and positive must be said about that.

We have spent a long time covering rough ground, and it may well seem that we do not have very many positive results to show for our effort. I have argued, along the way, that for Spinoza substance is defined simply as that which is independent of external causes, that Spinoza identifies substance and attribute, that he probably does not identify substance with the whole of Nature, and that on his view whatever is in itself must be conceived through itself (and vice versa). But my main concern has been a negative one: to show, not only that there is serious disagreement among Spinoza scholars even about fundamental matters of interpretation, but also that two of the most prominent and plausible lines of interpretation rest on very shaky foundations.

These polemics were necessary, I think, to pave the way for what is to come. In the remainder of this book I shall be striking out in a different direction, to propound an interpretation which in some ways is quite radical. I shall not often look back over my shoulder to see what others have done. And I shall not be able to prove that my way is the only way of reading Spinoza. But it does seem to me that any responsible critic must take very seriously the difficulties alternative interpretations face and ask himself how he would deal differently with the texts.

To begin with, then, it seems to me that the most important and interesting thing which philosophers have tried to do is no less than this, namely: To give a general description of the *whole* of the Universe, mentioning all the most important kinds of things which we *know* to be in it, considering how far it is likely that there are in it important kinds of things which we do not absolutely *know* to be in it, and also considering the most important ways in which these various kinds of things are related to one another.

—G. E. Moore, *Some Main Problems of Philosophy,* "What Is Philosophy?"

# 2   The Causality of God

# First Thoughts and Difficulties

The problem of determining what Spinoza means when he says that God is the cause of all things is as difficult as it is important. I will begin by stating certain things that are rather vague, and perhaps obvious, but I hope undeniable. I shall then construct a theory which I think fits these facts and explains a number of others as well. The result will be an interpretation of Spinoza which, though neither obvious nor undeniable, is nonetheless fairly precise and supported by considerable evidence.

There is perhaps no catchword of Spinozistic criticism more familiar than the contention that Spinoza assimilates the relation of causality to the relation of logical implication. And no doubt anything said so often must have some justification. In this case, the justification is twofold. First, as we have noted earlier, when Spinoza wants to characterize the relation between substance and mode, beyond saying that modes exist in and are conceived through substance, he says that God is the cause of the things that are in him, that he has produced them or determined them, or that they *follow* from him. This last form of expression, which is the most definite, is strongly suggestive of the relation of logical implication.

Second, Spinoza often elaborates these statements by appealing to a geometrical analogy. Thus, in the scholium to $E$ Ip17 he writes that "from the supreme power of God, or from his infinite nature, infinite things in infinite ways, that is, all things, have necessarily flowed out or always follow by the same necessity, and in the same way as from the nature of a triangle it follows, from eternity and to eternity, that its three angles equal two right angles" (II:62). Here, as in many other places, Spinoza seems to be saying, as clearly as we could possibly wish, that the causal relation between God and the things that are in him is not merely a necessary relation, but a relation whose necessity is logical.

Statements of this sort have caused no end of trouble. Confronted with the claim that "things proceed from God as the properties of a

triangle proceed from its nature," Leibniz complained that "there is
no analogy between essences and existing things." What this suggests
is that the relation of logical implication is one which obtains only between essences, that it makes no sense to speak of its obtaining between
existing things. And this is a criticism with which we may well sympa-
thize, though we might now prefer to say that relations of logical implication hold between propositions, or statements, rather than essences.

Moreover, as Spinoza insists in the passage quoted above, the relation
of logical implication is a timeless one. God's causality, therefore, must
also be timeless—or as Spinoza puts it, "God's omnipotence has been
actual from eternity and will remain in the same actuality to eternity"
($E$ Ip17s, II:62). This being the case, it is extremely difficult to see
how Spinoza could ever allow for the possibility of change. Indeed,
this is one reason why some of his interpreters have been so bold as
to assert that for Spinoza the phenomenal world, in which things come
into being and pass away is an illusion.

Again, many of Spinoza's interpreters have felt that, if all things do
follow from God in this way, then it ought to be possible, in principle,
to deduce the existence of particular finite beings from the existence
of the Infinite Being. Spinoza does not carry out any such deduction,
which has been variously interpreted as a flaw in the system or as a
natural defect of human knowledge.[1]

These criticisms may or may not be well founded. It would be rash
at this point to say very much about a matter that has such far-reaching
implications. But this much may be said with certainty: Spinoza con-
ceives the causal relation between substance and its modes to be in
some way analogous to the logical relation between ground and
consequent.

Now it may be noticed that I have spoken of this causal relation
as a relation between substance and its modes, but that Spinoza often
speaks of it as a relation between God's nature or essence and the things
which follow from that nature or essence. Thus, in $E$ Ip16 infinite numbers of things are said to follow "from the necessity of the divine nature."

In the demonstration of *E* Ip33, Spinoza paraphrases this by saying
that "all things have necessarily followed from the given nature of God."
We are given another paraphrase of the same proposition in the demonstration of *E* Ip17 when Spinoza writes that infinite numbers of things
follow "from the laws of the divine nature." In the passage quoted
above, things were said to follow from God's "infinite nature" or from
his "supreme power"—phrases that are made explicitly equivalent by
*E* Ip34, where Spinoza declares that "the power of God is his essence
itself." He also speaks of things as following from the divine attributes
(*E* Ip29s) and from the absolute nature of the divine attributes (*E*
Ip21), though this last form of expression seems to be applied only
to the infinite modes and not to all things. All of these phrases, except
the last, appear to be used equivalently, with the result that we can
say indifferently of things that they follow from God, or from his nature,
or from his power, or from the laws of his nature, or from his attributes.

The next thing to be observed is that in many places Spinoza expresses
a very strong belief in the possibility of explaining all events in terms
of scientific laws. Writing "Of Miracles" in his *Theological-Political
Treatise,* he contends that every event in nature is determined by natural
laws. "Nothing happens in nature which would contradict its universal
laws, nor does anything occur which does not agree with them or follow
from them" (*TTP* vi, III:83). By a law, here, he appears to have
in mind a regularity in nature. "The term 'law,' taken absolutely, signi-
fies that according to which each individual, or all or some members of
the same species, act in one and the same fixed and definite manner"
(*TTP* iv, III:57).

Because he thinks all events are determined by laws of this sort, Spinoza denies that there can be such a thing as a miracle—if by "miracle"
is meant an event which cannot, in principle, be referred to some regularity in nature. Where an event cannot be referred to any known regularity, it will no doubt seem very strange and mysterious to us. And
if we are superstitious, we may say that it defies natural explanation.
But this is both an intellectual mistake, since all things have natural

causes, and a mark of impiety rather than piety, for reasons we shall
soon discover.

First, however, we should point out, in view of the things that have
often been said about Spinoza by his commentators, that when Spinoza
speaks of things as having natural causes, he does not appear to have
anything very esoteric in mind. Discussing the crossing of the Red Sea
by the Jews escaping from Egypt, for example, he suggests that a way
was opened for them "by an east wind which blew very strongly all
night," adducing Exodus 14:21 in evidence. Again, in the case where
God is said to have changed the hearts of the Egyptians, so that they
hated the Israelites (Psalm 105:24), Spinoza argues that this too was
a natural change, since we find in Exodus 1 that the Egyptians had
"no slight reason for . . . reducing the Israelites to slavery." Exodus
tells us, what the Psalm does not, that the Egyptians feared the growing
numbers and power of the Jews. That Scripture refers such events directly to God, not always mentioning the attendant circumstances which
would provide a natural explanation, results from the desire for edifica-
tion. Scripture's aim is "only to narrate what seizes the popular imagination, and to do so in that method and style which best serve to arouse
wonder and consequently to impress the minds of the masses with devo-
tion" (*TTP* vi, III:90). But though it may not always be mentioned
by Scripture, there is always a natural cause of the sort indicated.

Note that Spinoza speaks of the laws of nature in the same logical
language that he uses of God's power or essence. Nothing happens in
nature that does not *follow* from her universal laws. This suggests that
there may be some very close connection between the laws of nature
and God's power or essence—a suggestion which is confirmed by passages
both in the *Theological-Political Treatise* and in the *Ethics*. In the
former work, Spinoza writes:

> By the guidance of God I understand the fixed and immutable
> order of nature, or concatenation of natural things; for the universal
> laws of nature, according to which all things happen and are deter-

mined, are nothing but the eternal decrees of God, which always
involve eternal truth and necessity. Therefore, whether we say that
all things happen according to the laws of nature, or whether we
say that they are governed by the decree and guidance of God,
we say the same thing. Because the power of all natural things is
nothing but the power itself of God, through which alone all things
happen and are determined. (*TTP* iii, III:45–46)

Again, in the *Ethics,* Spinoza writes that:

Nothing happens in nature which could be attributed to any defect
in it, for nature is always and everywhere one and the same. Its
virtue and its power of acting are the same—that is, the laws and
rules of nature, according to which all things happen and are
changed from one form to another, are always and everywhere
the same. And therefore there must also be one and the same ground
for understanding the nature of things of any kind whatever,
namely, the universal laws and rules of nature. (*E* III pref., II:138)

In these passages it seems clear enough that Spinoza is, somehow, identifying the power or essence of God or Nature with the scientific laws that
govern phenomena. This is why it is impious to believe in miracles.
To deny that things have a natural explanation is to deny the power
of God. Belief in miracles, paradoxically, is atheism. Conversely, so far
as we achieve an understanding of how Nature works according to
eternal laws, we increase our knowledge of God.

Here, I contend, we have a key to understanding those passages in
which Spinoza speaks of things as following from God's nature. For
things to follow from the necessity of the divine nature, for them to
exist in and be conceived through the one substance, is for them to
be determined by and intelligible in terms of scientific laws. This much,
I think, must be admitted on any interpretation of Spinoza's metaphysics.
But it may be that we can go a good deal further and say something

much more definite about the relation between substance and its modes, something which will, if it is correct, clarify a number of very obscure passages in Spinoza's writings.

## The Model Metaphysic

Let me begin by sketching a metaphysic of a type which will be familiar to all who have studied the British philosophy of the early years of this century. Perhaps no one has ever advanced this particular metaphysic, but many people have held views about the nature of the universe which were, at least, expressed in these categories. I shall then explore the possibility of understanding Spinoza's system in terms of this model metaphysic, although it is obviously described by him in a very different way.

Suppose we have a set of propositions—call it $A$—which constitutes a complete and accurate description of the world of extended objects, a description that includes propositions stating whatever is, or has been, or will be the case with respect to such objects. It may be that a really complete description is impossible, not merely because there are indefinitely many objects to describe, but because objects may be classified, and hence described, in indefinitely many ways. Nevertheless, we can at least say what logical kinds of proposition would have to be contained in any description of this world that professed to be complete.

There would be singular propositions, like "This table is three feet long" and "The Earth revolves in an elliptical orbit around the Sun." These attribute a property to an object or state that some relation holds between two or more objects. And there would be general propositions, like "All planets have elliptical orbits" and "Some bodies are three feet long." These attribute a property or a relation to all or some members of some class of individual objects.

General propositions are a mixed but interesting lot. The fundamental distinction to be drawn among them is not the distinction between universal generalizations, which are of the form "All $F$ is $G$," and particular generalizations, which are of the form "Some *F* is *G*," but rather the distinction between nomological and accidental generalizations.

The distinguishing characteristic of nomological propositions is their strict universality: they are universal propositions, stating something about all members of some class of objects, and that class is not defined with reference to some particular time and place. For example, "Every body not acted on by an external force continues in its state of rest or uniform motion in a straight line." Nomological propositions are commonly known as "laws of nature." But this latter designation is ambiguous and has misleading associations, so that it is perhaps best avoided.

Accidental generalizations are all those which are not nomological, either because they are not universal, like "Some bodies are three feet long," or because, though universal, they are not strictly universal, in that the class of which they are true is defined with reference to some particular time and place. For example, "All of the objects in my room on the 1st of May weighed less than 150 pounds." The designation of such propositions as accidental is, as we shall see, also misleading; but it is well entrenched, there is no handy substitute, and there is, as we shall also see, some justice in the designation.

The defining characteristic of nomological propositions is their strict universality. But there is another characteristic which follows from this: that they are necessarily true, that they could not have been otherwise. Only necessary propositions are true without spatial or temporal limitation. Necessity and strict universality are indissolubly linked. So nomological generalizations are, and accidental generalizations are not, necessary truths.

As a result, nomological generalizations do, though accidental generlizations do not, support counterfactual inference. The principle of inertia, given above as an example of a nomological generalization—if, indeed, it is a genuine law of nature, a true nomological proposition—could not have been otherwise. Consequently, if my pen, which in fact is now acted on by my hand, were not acted on by any external force, it would continue in a state of rest or uniform motion in a straight line.

By contrast, the (true) generalization that "All of the objects in my room on the 1st of May weighed less than 150 pounds" could have been otherwise and does not support counterfactual claims of the kind that laws do. I was not in fact in my room on the 1st of May. But suppose I had been. It would then follow, not that I would have weighed less than 150 pounds, but that not all of the objects in my room on the 1st of May weighed less than 150 pounds. Weight-losing, alas, is not that easy.

For our present purposes, however, the most important characteristic of nomological propositions is that they are not reducible to conjunctions or disjunctions of singular propositions. Accidental generalizations are. When I say that all of the objects in my room on the 1st of May weighed less than 150 pounds, my statement may be viewed as equivalent to: "This object, which was in my room on the 1st of May, weighed less than 150 pounds, and that object, which was in my room on the 1st of May, weighed less than 150 pounds and . . ." and so on, through a complete enumeration of the objects in my room on that day. Once I have said, of each of the objects in my room on that day, that it weighed less than 150 pounds, I do not add anything further by going on to say that they all weighed less than 150 pounds.

With nomological propositions it is different. There the notion of a complete enumeration is out of place. A strictly universal generalization is, in principle, an assertion about an infinite number of individual objects. It cannot be replaced without loss by any finite conjunction of singular statements. Hence, if we were giving a complete description of the world, we would need to include nomological generalizations as separate items. But we would not need to include accidental generalizations. They would be redundant.

Because there are general propositions in our description, the propositions making up the set A are not logically independent of one another. Some follow logically from others, with the result that you could not consistently deny them without denying some one of the propositions from which they follow. For example, suppose it is true that

(1)  Any body which is near another body with a mass of 5.975 $\times$ 10²⁴ kgm and a radius of 6.371 $\times$ 10⁶ m and which starts from rest and falls freely toward the other body for one second falls a distance of 4.9 m.

and that

(2)  Body *a* was near another body with a mass of 5.975 $\times$ 10²⁴ kgm and a radius of 6.371 $\times$ 10⁶ m and it started from rest and fell freely toward the other body for one second.

and that

(3)  Body *a* fell 4.9 m.

(3) follows logically from (1) and (2)—you could not consistently deny (3) without denying either (1) or (2). But if there were no general propositions in *A*, and hence no propositions like (1), then presumably (2) and (3) would be logically independent of one another. Either one could be consistently denied without denying the other.

Not only is it the case that some propositions in *A* follow from others, but every singular proposition in *A* will follow from other propositions in *A* in the way that (3) follows from (1) and (2). It will follow from a law, or set of laws, together with a statement of antecedent conditions. Among the nomological propositions, there is another kind of logical interdependence. They can be organized into a deductive system, such that, given a few of them as axioms, the rest can be derived as theorems.

Thus, in our complete description of the world, the ideal of a unified science is realized. Every true singular proposition about extended objects has its scientific explanation, and every nomological proposition has its place in a system analogous to Newton's *Principia*.

The world, of course, mirrors our description of it. As the Philosopher says, the world is everything that is the case, it is the totality of facts, not of things. For it is in virtue of the existence of facts that propositions are true. If the proposition that "this table weighs fifty pounds" is true, then it is true because there is, in the world, the fact this proposition describes. If it is not true, that is because the fact this proposition purports to describe does not exist. No doubt the table exists, too, but after we have mentioned the fact of which it is a constituent it would be superfluous to mention the table as well.

For every distinct kind of proposition, there is a distinct kind of fact. As there are singular propositions, so there are singular facts. As, among general propositions, the accidental ones are, and the nomological ones are not, equivalent to conjunctions or disjunctions of singular propositions, so, among facts, those to which true accidental generalizations correspond are simply sets of singular facts, whereas those to which true nomological generalizations correspond are general nomological facts. And as, among nomological propositions, some are axioms and others theorems, so some nomological facts are basic and others derivative.

Needless to say, facts are not independent of one another. It is not the case that any one could be different and everything else remain the same. This is a consequence of the existence of general nomological facts. They provide the causal nexus which justifies the inference from the existence of one singular fact to the existence of another. The singular fact that body $a$ fell 4.9 m. is causally dependent on the singular fact that it started from rest and fell freely for one second toward a body having such-and-such mass and radius and the general nomological fact that this is what bodies do under those conditions.

In general, wherever there is a relation of logical dependence among propositions, there is a relation of causal dependence among the corresponding facts. Thus, the world is thoroughly deterministic. Every singular fact depends on other singular facts and on nomological facts. And the derivative nomological facts, like that described by Galileo's law for freely falling bodies, depend on the basic nomological facts. The only facts that are independent of all others are these basic nomological facts.

Such is the picture of the world with which our model metaphysic presents us. Whether or not this is a correct "general description of the whole of the Universe," I am not prepared to say. Anyone who is familiar with the sources from which I have drawn in putting together this rather eclectic view, who has read, say, Russell's *Lectures on Logical Atomism,* or Ludwig Wittgenstein's *Tractatus,* or Karl Popper's *Logic of Scientific Discovery,* will recognize immediately that nearly every one of the doctrines I have stated so dogmatically is highly controversial. But that does not matter. For I am not primarily interested in the truth of this view. What I am primarily interested in is the possibility of using it to help us understand Spinoza. I must add, however, that I think some of these doctrines are more defensible than they are often given credit for being, and that I shall have something to say in their defense in the next chapter.

## Application of the Model Metaphysic to Spinoza

Suppose we make the following correlation between this system and Spinoza's: we identify the basic nomological facts with the attribute of extension, the derivative nomological facts with the infinite and eternal modes of that attribute, and the singular facts with Spinoza's finite modes. The facts described by accidental generalizations, since they are (sets of) singular facts, will also be finite modes. Does this shed any light at all on the "difficulties and impenetrable abstractions" of Spinoza's system? I think it does.

Let us take first the identification of the basic nomological facts with the divine attribute of extension. What evidence is there for this, and what problem does it help us to solve? To begin with, there is the point made above, that Spinoza somehow equates the power or essence of God with the laws that govern phenomena. What I wish to say now is that the equation is rather with the general facts that the most fundamental of those laws describe. This distinction between a law and the feature of reality that the law describes—what Popper would call a "structural property of the world"—is not always strictly maintained, even among contemporary philosophers. Witness Arthur Lovejoy, who speaks in *The Great Chain of Being* of "those generalized facts which we call empirical laws" (p. 148). But I think the distinction will turn out to be a useful one. Where Spinoza says that "the attributes of God express eternal and infinite essence" (*E* ID6), we will read this as roughly equivalent to his statement that the laws of nature "according to which all things are changed from one form to another, are everywhere and always the same" (*E* III pref., II:138). The laws of nature, being strictly universal propositions, describe facts that are present throughout all of space and time.

Part of the justification for talking about facts, rather than things, lies in Spinoza's doctrine that every idea involves an element of affirmation (*E* IIP49). If, for example, we have an idea of a triangle, then that idea involves the affirmation that the sum of its interior angles is equal to 180 degrees. Thus Hampshire comments in his *Spinoza* that

> The word "idea" is used so widely in Spinoza as to include what we would normally call an "assertion" or "proposition"; deliberately, and in opposition to Descartes, he makes no distinction between "having an idea" and "asserting" or "making a statement." So an idea in his sense may be qualified as true or false, and one idea may be said to follow logically from another; in normal usage we speak only of propositions or assertions as true or false, or as following logically from each other. (p. 66)

Whether Spinoza's use of the term "idea" is farther than Descartes' from "the normal use" of that highly ambiguous term we need not say. But this does suggest that the correlate, in the attribute of extension, of a Spinozistic idea, that with which a true idea must agree, its ideatum (*E* IA6), ought to be a fact involving an extended object, rather than an extended object itself.

Suppose we apply this doctrine to the attribute of extension. We have an idea of extension. That idea will involve certain affirmations about extended things, for there are certain respects in which all bodies agree

($E$ IIL2, II:98). The affirmations involved in our idea of extension attribute these common properties to extended things and so describe the nature of extension. Such affirmations are general propositions of the form: everything which has the attribute of extension has also common property $X$. What I am contending is that these propositions, included by Spinoza among the "common notions," are for him the fundamental laws of nature, and that the facts they describe constitute the nature of the attribute of extension.

This conception of things has a fruitful application to the interpretation of Spinoza's statements concerning our knowledge of God. If we regard the nature of the divine attribute of extension as made up of a set of facts described by general propositions about all things having that attribute, then I think we are in a better position to understand how Spinoza can claim so confidently that the human mind has an adequate knowledge of the eternal and infinite essence of God ($E$ IIP47). This proposition must surely have shocked Spinoza's contemporaries. Even today, Spinoza's readers ought to be taken aback by it. For viewed as a doctrine in the realm of natural theology, rather than as a thesis about our knowledge of the foundations of science, it is one of Spinoza's most radical departures from his predecessors.

But reflect. Spinoza tells us that each man has adequate knowledge of the common notions ($E$ IIP38–39). We are assuming that the facts which the common notions describe constitute the nature of the attribute of extension. The attribute of extension is one of the attributes that constitute the essence of God. Hence, in knowing the common notions, man knows the nature of extension. In having adequate knowledge of the nature of extension, he has adequate knowledge of the essence of God.

This view will be confirmed, I think, if we look at the rather brief proof Spinoza gives of this proposition:

> $E$ IIP47: The human mind has an adequate knowledge of the eternal and infinite essence of God.
> Dem: The human mind possesses ideas (IIP22) from which

(IIP23) it perceives itself and its own body (IIP19), and external bodies as actually existing. Therefore (IIP45–46) it has an adequate knowledge of the eternal and infinite essence of God. Q.E.D.

Anyone who is at all surprised by the proposition itself should be astounded by the casual way it is proved. Nevertheless, on this interpretation it is intelligible enough. The key proposition is IIP45, according to which "every idea of every body, or of every singular thing actually existing, necessarily involves the eternal and infinite essence of God." I think we can easily see why this is so. The common properties which appear on an analysis of the nature of extension are called common because they are present in every body. Hence, every idea of every body will involve them. That is, every idea of every body will involve the affirmation that that body has common property $X$. And this affirmation is simply an instance of the general proposition that every extended thing is an $X$, which is one of the propositions describing the nature of the attribute of extension.

So far I have been attempting to justify taking the attribute of extension to be a set of facts described by certain fundamental laws of nature known as common notions. What of the infinite modes? I said above that they were also to be regarded as sets of nomological facts, though derivative ones. What evidence is there for this?

Let us take first $E$ Ip21. There Spinoza says that "all things which follow from the absolute nature of any attribute of God must always exist and be infinite." The "things which follow" are generally spoken of as the infinite modes. Later, in $E$ Ip22 and $E$ Ip23, Spinoza distinguishes between infinite modes which follow immediately from the absolute nature of a divine attribute and those which follow mediately, through some other infinite mode. Hence we have two sorts of infinite mode: the immediate and the mediate. Spinoza does not give us, in the *Ethics,* any examples of infinite modes, nor does he tell us how many there are supposed to be under any given attribute. But he does give examples in the *Short Treatise* and in one of the letters, and it is usually thought that there will be one immediate infinite mode and one mediate infinite mode under each attribute.

One way of approaching Spinoza's doctrine of infinite modes is to ask in what sense they might be thought to "follow" from their respective attributes. Their relation to the attributes cannot be one of temporal succession because both terms of the relation are eternal. Nor can it, on the face of things, be a relation of logical consequence, for that is a relation which holds between propositions, and not between things (or facts). Nevertheless, the relation of logical consequence, being one which holds timelessly, is clearly closer to what Spinoza has in mind than the relation of temporal successsion. Let us say tentatively that it is a relation of causal dependence between general facts, which is the counterpart in the order of things (more accurately, the order of facts) of a relation of logical consequence in the order of ideas (more accurately, the order of propositions). On this interpretation, Spinoza's thesis that every infinite and eternal mode of the attribute of extension follows either directly from the absolute nature of the attribute of extension or indirectly from some other infinite mode which follows from the nature of extension (*E* Ip23)—put in logical terms—amounts to the thesis that every scientific law relating to extended objects can be derived either directly from the fundamental laws governing extended objects or from a finite series of nomological propositions which terminates ultimately in the fundamental laws.

Spinoza does not give us much information about what the infinite modes are, but the information we are given provides an interesting confirmation of the claim made here. We want to say that all other scientific laws follow logically from some set of propositions stating properties common to all bodies. Now in *Ep.* 64, when Spinoza is asked to give an example of something that is produced immediately by God, he mentions, under the attribute of extension, motion-and-rest. As a result, motion-and-rest has acquired the title of immediate infinite and eternal mode under the attribute of extension, which is to say that it is identified with what follows immediately from the absolute nature

of the attribute of extension. But we are not told any more about motion-and-rest than this and there has been a great deal of uncertainty
about the meaning of Spinoza's doctrine of infinite modes.

On the interpretation being put forward here, we will understand
this in the following way. Our idea of motion-and-rest involves certain
affirmations about things which are in motion or at rest, such as the
principle of inertia. It should be at least theoretically possible to deduce
the general propositions which express these affirmations from the general
propositions involved in our idea of extension, that is, to deduce the
laws of motion from the nature of extended things. To say that these
laws of motion can be deduced from the common notions is equivalent
to saying that the infinite mode of motion-and-rest "follows" from or
depends causally on the absolute nature of the attribute of extension.
This immediate infinite mode will consist of that set of general facts
which are described by the laws of motion.

I think Spinoza would have regarded such a deduction as in principle
possible, even if he was not prepared to supply the details of it himself.
In fact, it seems that we are given a sample of what this deduction
would be like in the axioms and lemmas which occur between propositions 13 and 14 of part II. Spinoza starts out by remarking that it
is necessary for him to say something about the nature of bodies, that
is, something about the nature of extended things. He then posits two
axioms:

A1: All bodies are either in motion or at rest.
A2: Every body moves, now more slowly, now more quickly.
    (II:97)

That these axioms would be numbered among the common notions
is clear from the proof of lemma 2:

L2: All bodies agree in certain things.
Dem: For all bodies agree in this, that they involve the
conception of one and the same attribute (IID1), that they are

capable of motion at one time quicker and at another slower.
(II:97)

Shortly after this, in the first corollary, Spinoza claims that "it follows that a body in motion will continue in motion until it be determined to rest by another body, and that a body at rest will continue at rest until it be determined to motion by another body" (II:98). Here then we have a proposition about bodies in motion or at rest, a form of the familiar principle of inertia. This proposition is supposed to be deduced from a few propositions about bodies in general. The details of the deduction may not be convincing. It may, for example, involve assumptions other than the axioms, such as *E* Ip28. But the occurrence of this deduction suggests that, at the least, Spinoza would not have regarded the doctrine I have attributed to him as implausible.

On this interpretation, the "face of the whole universe," given by Spinoza as an example of something which follows from the attribute of extension as modified in an infinite mode (*Ep*. 64, IV:278), would refer to the sum of those other general facts which depend causally on the nature of extension. What the corresponding laws might be, and how they might be deduced from the nature of extension, we cannot say. But this is hardly surprising. If I am right, we are dealing here with a part of Spinoza's philosophy that is on the border between philosophy and science. It is quite natural that Spinoza should tell us little about the infinite modes.[2]

It is worth comparing the treatment of the infinite modes in the *Ethics* with that in the earlier *Short Treatise*. In both works the fundamental division of nature is into the attributes (*natura naturans*) and the modes (*natura naturata*) which depend on those attributes. But whereas in the *Ethics* Spinoza divides *natura naturata* into infinite modes and finite modes, in the *Short Treatise* the division is into general modes, which depend immediately on God, and particular modes, that is, all the "particular things which are produced by the general mode" (*KV* I, viii, I:47).

Of the general modes, Spinoza says that we know only two: motion in matter and the understanding in the thinking thing. The face of the whole universe is not named here. And though motion is said to be both infinite and eternal, these characteristics are put forward as ones which it is not Spinoza's business *as a philosopher* to explain:

> As for what particularly concerns motion, since it belongs more properly in a treatise on natural science, rather than here, to show that it has been from all eternity and will remain immutable for all eternity, that it is infinite in its kind, that through itself it can neither be nor be understood, but only by means of extension, all of these things I shall not treat here. I shall merely say this about it, that it is a Son, product, or effect, created immediately by God. (*KV* I, ix, I:48)

In a footnote Spinoza explains that what is said here about motion is not said "seriously. For the Author still intends to discover the cause of it, as he has already done to some extent *a posteriori*." This suggests that at the time of writing the *Short Treatise* Spinoza nevertheless hoped to give an a priori foundation to those properties of motion whose explanation is said to belong more properly to "a treatise on natural science." When he came to write the *Ethics,* he evidently felt that he had succeeded in doing this, for the properties asserted without proof in the *Short Treatise* are there proved *more geometrico* and made the basis for a new classification.

If my interpretation is correct, Spinoza has roughly the same justification for calling these general modes infinite and eternal that he has for describing the attributes in this way. The general modes are facts described by general, nomological propositions—necessary propositions which are always and everywhere valid. Their infinitude and eternity is a function of their strict universality. Thus we have the picture presented on page 63.

With this picture as background, I think we may make some headway on the problem of the finite modes. In E Ip26, Spinoza says that any-

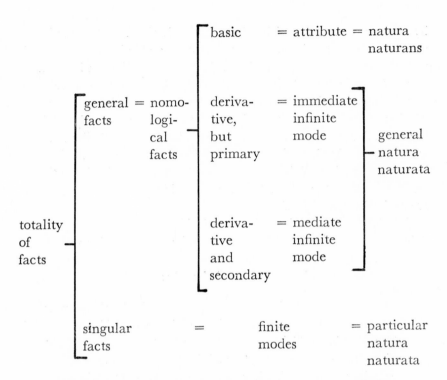

thing which "has been determined to any action has necessarily been so determined by God." But in E Ip28, he says that

> any singular thing, or any thing which is finite and has determinate existence, can neither exist nor be determined to action un- less . . . by another cause which is also finite and has a determinate existence; and again, this cause can neither exist nor be determined to action unless . . . by another cause which is also finite and determined to existence and action, and so on, *ad infinitum.*

Now this is difficult. God is not something finite. How is it that finite things are conditioned to act both by God and by something finite? From the proof of *E* Ip28, the answer appears to be that finite things are conditioned to exist and act by God only insofar as he is modified by "some modification which is finite." That is, the "something finite" mentioned in *E* Ip28 is a modification of God, and in being conditioned to act by something finite, a finite mode is conditioned to act by God.

But this will not do. In *E* Ip33, when Spinoza attempts to prove that "things could have been produced by God in no other manner and in no other order than that in which they have been produced," he argues that, if things had happened at all differently, God's nature would have had to be different, which is impossible. The order of events in nature must depend, in some way, on God's essence, that is, on the attributes, and not simply on God as modified in finite modes. So we are back where we started.

This difficulty was well put by Leibniz. Noting that, according to Spinoza, finite and temporal things cannot be produced "immediately" by an infinite cause (*E* Ip21), and that they are produced by other causes, individual and finite (*E* Ip28), he asks:

> How will they finally then spring from God? For they cannot come from him mediately, in this case, since we could never reach in this way things which are not similarly produced by another finite thing. It cannot, therefore, be said that God acts by mediating secondary causes, unless he produces secondary causes.[3]

What Spinoza's philosophy seems to require, for finite things, is both an infinite series of finite causes and a finite series of infinite causes terminating in God. It is difficult to see how these requirements are to be jointly satisfied.

I think that we have the materials at hand for an answer to this. Let me cast my approach in the form of a line by line commentary on the proof of *E* Ip28. I shall quote the individual sentences of the proof alternately with the translation into the logical form of my interpretation:

1. Whatever is determined to existence and action is thus determined by God (E Ip26 and Ip24c).

1a. Any proposition in *A* (except those which are axioms of scientific theory) must follow from other propositions in *A*.

2. But what is finite and has a determinate existence could not be produced by the absolute nature of any attribute of God, for whatever follows from the absolute nature of any attribute of God is infinite and eternal ($E$ Ip21).

2a. But a singular proposition cannot be deduced (solely) from the axioms of the scientific theory of $A$, for these are general propositions, and from general propositions alone only general propositions can be deduced.

3. The finite and determinate must therefore follow from God, or from some attribute of God, insofar as the latter is considered to be affected by some mode, for besides substance and modes, nothing exists ($E$ Ia1, Id3, Id5, and Ip25c).

3a. A singular proposition must then follow from propositions which are not axioms of the scientific theory of $A$, that is, from some theorem of the scientific theory of $A$, or from some singular proposition, for these are all the propositions there are in $A$.

4. But the finite and determinate also could not follow from God or from any one of his attributes, so far as that attribute is affected by a modification which is eternal and infinite ($E$ Ip22).

4a. But a singular proposition cannot be deduced (solely) from theorems of the scientific theory of $A$, for these too are general propositions.

5. It must, therefore, follow or be determined to existence and action by God, or by some attribute of God, insofar as the attribute is modified by a modification which is finite and has a determinate existence.

5a. The singular propositions of $A$ must then follow from other singular propositions of $A$ (taken together with some general propositions, for it is no more possible to deduce a singular conclusion from singular premises alone, than it is to deduce one from general premises alone).

Now, as the parenthetical additions show, the fit between Spinoza's words and my interpretation is not a perfect one. Nevertheless, the fit is close enough to be interesting, and if we read Spinoza as I think we should, the differences will turn out to be negligible.

What I propose is that we understand Spinoza as maintaining that finite things depend upon God both insofar as he is modified by finite modifications and insofar as he is modified by infinite modifications. To use a distinction that Spinoza introduces later (*E* IIID1), neither the infinite modes nor the finite modes are by themselves adequate causes of finite modes. Taken separately, they are only partial causes; the existence and actions of a particular finite mode cannot be understood either by reference to other finite modes alone or by reference to infinite modes alone, but only by reference to both infinite and finite modes.

Put in the language which I introduced earlier, this would be to say that the singular facts which exist at any given moment are determined by the previously existing singular facts and by certain general facts but that neither the previously existing singular facts nor the general facts alone suffice to determine what facts now exist. The previously existing singular facts give us the infinite series of finite causes. The general facts give us the finite series of infinite causes, terminating in God. This is the metaphysical equivalent of the logical or epistemological claim that propositions describing the existence and actions of particular things can be deduced from the laws of nature, if and only if the laws are taken together with a statement of antecedent conditions.

Spinoza never says, in so many words, that neither the infinite modes nor the finite modes are, by themselves, adequate causes of finite modes. But he does say a number of things which persuade me that this was his view. Consider first the passage in the *Treatise on the Correction of the Intellect* in which Spinoza discusses the relation between the fixed and eternal things, on the one hand, and the particular and mutable things, on the other. There Spinoza says that

> Above all it is necessary for us always to deduce all our ideas from physical things—that is, from real entities, proceeding, as far as we may, according to the series of causes, from one real entity

to another real entity . . . by the series of causes and real entities,
I understand here not the series of singular mutable things, but
only the series of fixed and eternal things. It would be impossible
for human weakness to grasp the series of singular mutable
things . . . nor is there any real need for us to understand their
series, since the essences of singular mutable things are not to be
drawn from their series or order of existence . . . the essence is
really sought solely from the fixed and eternal things, and from
the laws, inscribed in those things as in their true codes, according
to which all singular things occur and are ordered; indeed, these
singular mutable things depend so intimately . . . on the fixed
things that they can neither be nor be conceived without them.
(*TdIE*, 99–101, II:36–37)

This is an interesting and difficult passage. The singular mutable things
are naturally enough identified with the finite modes of the *Ethics;* but
there has been considerable speculation as to what the fixed and eternal
things might be.

It seems to me that Pollock is basically right in identifying them
with the infinite modes of the *Ethics* (though I suspect that we should
add the attributes as well). Note that the fixed and eternal things are
described, in a consciously metaphorical phrase, as having laws "inscribed" in them. These laws appear to be the laws of nature. We have,
then, an apparently finite series of eternal entities, somehow associated
with the laws of nature, on which the infinite series of particular things
depends very "intimately."

If we follow Pollock in identifying these things with the infinite modes,
and the interpretation I have been proposing in identifying the infinite
modes with the facts described by derivative nomological propositions,
then we have a fairly clear answer to the questions of what these eternal
entities are (they are nomological facts), and how they are associated
with the laws of nature (they are described by them), and how particular
things depend on them (for these nomological facts, in conjunction with

other singular facts, determine what singular facts exist at any given moment). The point is not that Spinoza thought explicitly in these categories. He did not. The point is that the concept of a nomological fact is the kind of concept that Spinoza's system seems to require, the kind of concept that he seems to be groping for or trying to express.

Pollock's comment is interesting in this connection. He asks:

> What can these eternal things be? The interpretation that lies nearest at hand for a modern reader is to identify them with the constant relations among phenomena which we now call laws of nature. But this is evidently not admissible. Spinoza, the down-right enemy of abstractions and universals, knew the difference between relations and things far too well to confuse them in this way. Besides, he wanted no artificial way of describing laws of nature; the name was already familiar in his time, and he could speak of them, when he thought fit, just as we do. In fact, he does speak of the "eternal things" as having laws of their own in some way attached to or involved in them, which pervade the whole world of phenomena. Clearly, therefore, the things in question are not themselves laws. (Pollock, pp. 150–151)

He then goes on to argue that they are the infinite modes. Now, that the eternal things are not the laws themselves, I agree. Pollock, however, provides no reason for thinking that they are not those general features of reality which the laws describe. While Spinoza has a natural way of referring to the laws, he does not have a natural way of referring to what the laws describe.

But—to return to our problem—what is of special interest here is the dependence of the singular mutable things on the fixed and eternal things. This seems to mean that the finite modes are determined to exist and act solely by the finite series of infinite modes, and to contradict *E* Ip28 of the *Ethics,* which seems to say that finite modes are determined to exist and act solely by an infinite series of other finite modes.

My view, however, is that these two passages are complementary, rather than contradictory. Neither the finite modes nor the infinite modes, by themselves, are adequate to determine the existence and actions of a particular finite mode. The difference between the *Ethics* and the *Treatise* is merely one of emphasis. In the *Ethics,* Spinoza is emphasizing the dependence of finite modes on other finite modes, whereas in the *Treatise,* he is emphasizing their dependence on the infinite modes. But in any causal explanation of one sort, there is an implicit reference to a causal explanation of the other sort. Whenever we explain a particular event by mentioning a law of nature under which it may be subsumed, we are implying the prior existence of appropriate antecedent conditions. And conversely, whenever we give as the explanation of some event its antecedent conditions, we are implying the existence of a law linking those conditions with that event. This, I think, may explain the otherwise rather puzzling remark that occurs in *Ep.* 40:

> For example, if someone asks by what cause a body determined in a certain way is moved, we may reply that it is determined to such a motion by another body, and this one again by another, and so on to infinity. This, I say, is a possible reply because the question is only about motion, and by continually positing another body, we assign a sufficient and eternal cause of its motion.
> (IV:198)

It is difficult to see how Spinoza could regard such a series of finite causes—even though it extends to infinity—as an *eternal* cause of such a motion. Neither the series nor its individual members are eternal entities in Spinoza's usage of that term, for according to *E* ID8, by "eternity" Spinoza understands

> existence itself, so far as it is conceived to follow necessarily from the definition alone of the eternal thing.

>    Explanation: For such existence, like the essence of the thing, is
>    conceived as an eternal truth. It cannot, therefore, be explained by
>    duration or time, even if the duration be conceived without begin-
>    ning or end.

Since the essences of these finite things do not involve existence, the
things are not eternal. And judging from the final remark in the explanation of the definition, the fact that their series extends to infinity would
be irrelevant. The only thing I can see that could be regarded as an
eternal cause here would be the law governing the series—presumably
that would be the principle of inertia—or rather, the nomological fact
described by that law.

To say that the infinite and finite modes are separately necessary
and only jointly sufficient conditions of finite modes does, I think, give
us a plausible way of reconciling what looks like an outright contradiction
in Spinoza's metaphysics. This interpretation is supported by other things
which Spinoza says. Let us begin by considering the note he appends
to *E* Ip28:

>    Since certain things must have been produced by God immediately,
>    that is, those which necessarily follow from his absolute nature,
>    these primary products being the mediating cause for those [*NS*:
>    other] things which, nevertheless, without God can neither be nor
>    be conceived, it follows first, that of the things immediately pro-
>    duced by him, God is the proximate cause absolutely. [*NS*: I say
>    the proximate cause absolutely and] not in their own kind, as they
>    say; for the effects of God can neither be nor be conceived without
>    their cause. (*E* Ip15 and Ip24c)
>    It follows, second, that God cannot properly be called the remote
>    cause of singular things, unless to distinguish them from the things
>    which he has immediately produced, *or rather which follow from
>    his absolute nature*. For by a remote cause we understand one which
>    is in no way conjoined to its effect. But all things which are, are

in God, and so depend on him that without him they can neither be nor be conceived. [My italics]

This is a passage concerning which there may be some difference of opinion, but whose general drift seems clear enough. God is asserted to be the proximate cause of the things he has produced immediately. It is denied that he is the remote cause of singular things, in the peculiar sense where a remote cause would "in no way be conjoined to its effect." But it is implied that God is the remote cause of individual things in a more natural sense, namely, that he is their cause through the mediation of the things which he has produced immediately.

At first glance, we might suppose that the things which God has immediately produced would be only the immediate infinite modes. That is what the phrase, taken by itself, naturally suggests, and some interpreters have thought that they are obviously referred to. But Spinoza also identifies the things in question as "those which follow from the absolute nature of God," a description which clearly has a broader denotation, since it is used by Spinoza to refer to all the infinite modes and not merely to those which follow immediately from his absolute nature (see *E* Ip23 and its dem.). Moreover, it appears from the clause italicized that Spinoza regards the first description as likely to mislead. So I think we may take the things immediately produced by God to be *all* the infinite modes.

On this reading, Spinoza's doctrine is that (1) God is the proximate cause of the infinite modes, (2) God is the remote cause of the finite modes, in the sense that he is their cause through the mediation of the infinite modes. This will agree with the *Short Treatise,* according to which

God is the proximate cause of the things that are infinite and immutable, and which we say have been created immediately by him, but in a sense, he is the remote cause of all particular things. (*KV* I, iii, I:36)

> The general [*natura naturata*] consists of all the modes which
> depend immediately on God . . . the particular [*natura naturata*]
> consists of all the particular things which are produced by the general
> mode. (*KV* I, viii, I:47)

The *Short Treatise*, it should be noted, knows no distinction between
immediate and mediate infinite modes.

This confirms my contention that the infinite modes are at least a
partial cause of the finite modes—and also, incidentally, strengthens the
identification of the infinite modes with the fixed and eternal things
of the *Treatise on the Correction of the Intellect,* which,

> though they are singular . . . on account of their presence and
> power everywhere, will be to us like universals, or the genera of defi-
> nitions of singular mutable things. *They will be the proximate causes
> of all things.* (*TdIE*, 101, II:37)

But the infinite modes cannot be an adequate cause of finite modes.
For if they were, the finite modes, like the infinite modes, would follow
from the absolute nature of God, and we know that nothing finite can
follow from the absolute nature of God (*E* Ip21).

In the *Short Treatise* Spinoza expresses this view more clearly than
in any other place. There he distinguishes between a principal cause,
which "produces an effect by virtue of its own powers alone, without
the aid of anything else" and a subsidiary cause (*causa minus princi-
palis*), which "is merely one condition or factor which is necessary but
not adequate to produce a certain effect."[4] God, Spinoza says,

> is a principal cause of his works which he has created immediately,
> such as motion in matter, in which a subsidiary cause can have
> no place, since it is always confined to particular things, as when
> he dries the sea through a strong wind, and similarly with all par-
> ticular things in nature. (*KV* I, iii, I:35–36)

That is, God is the principal (or in the terminology of the *Ethics,* adequate) cause of the infinite modes. But of the finite modes, he is a subsidiary (or partial) cause—at least, in so far as he is infinite. In the realm of the finite, other finite modes are also required as subsidiary causes.

We may take this, then, as our answer to Leibniz' question: How do things "finally spring from God"? We will not get back to God by following up the infinite chain of finite causes. Even if we could do that, it would not lead us in the right direction. But we will get back to God by following the equally necessary finite chain of infinite causes.

What is perhaps of more interest is that in recognizing that God is not, in so far as he is infinite, the adequate cause of finite things, we have also an answer to that very bothersome puzzle about the relation of God's causality to time and change, an answer which we can let Spinoza give in his own words. In the second dialogue of the *Short Treatise,* Spinoza has one of the characters, Erasmus, raise an objection to the author's spokesman, Theophilus, of a sort which almost makes one think that Spinoza had foreknowledge of what historians of philosophy would later write about him. Erasmus speaks:

> You said . . . that the effect of an inner cause cannot perish so long as its cause lasts. This, indeed, I see to be certainly true. But if this is so, then how can God be an inner cause of all things, since many things perish? (*KV* I, ii, I:33)

But Erasmus is more alert than most historians of philosophy, and he is able to answer this one himself:

> But you will say, according to your previous distinction [between principal and subsidiary causes], that God is properly a cause of the effects which he has produced immediately by his attributes alone, without any further circumstances, and that these cannot cease

to be as long as their cause endures, but that you do not call God an inner cause of the effects whose essence does not depend on him immediately, but which come to be through another thing (except insofar as their causes neither do, nor can, act without God, or outside him). And, therefore, since they are not produced by God immediately, they can cease to be.

The things produced immediately by God, which here, as in the *Short Treatise* generally and in *E* Ip28s, are *all* of the infinite modes, share the eternal nature of their cause. For God, insofar as he is infinite, is their adequate cause. The things not produced immediately by God, particular or finite things, are not eternal; they do come into being and pass away. For God is their adequate cause, not insofar as he is infinite, but only insofar as he is modified both by finite and by infinite modifications. Finite modes require, as their partial cause, other finite modes and hence do not share the eternal nature of their cause.

Similarly, there is no problem in Spinoza of deducing the finite from the infinite. Spinoza does not, as John Caird would have it, try and fail to make the deduction. Nor does he, as Joachim would have it, abstain from the attempt because he knows the limitations of the finite human intellect. Deducing the finite *solely* from the infinite, in his philosophy, is in principle impossible. Even an infinite intellect could not do it. Thus, though Spinoza does certainly assimilate the relation of causality to that of logical implication, he does not do this in a way which would have the disastrous consequences usually thought to follow from such a step.

## The Interpretation of the Definitions of Substance and Mode

In the preceding chapter I argued that the relation of mode to substance is one of causal dependence. Modes exist in substance in the sense that they are causally dependent on substance; substance exists in itself in the sense that it is not causally dependent on anything else. But to say only this, as I pointed out, is to say something very vague. The notion of causal dependence used here must be clarified before we can be said to have an interpretation of Spinoza's language which is at all definite. Until we have some analysis of God's causality, the connotations of the terms "substance" and "mode" are very uncertain.

Toward the end of the chapter, moreover, I suggested that there might be some difficulty about the denotations of these terms. "Mode" denotes, in part at any rate, such familiar individual things as me, you, the desk in my office, and so forth. But its denotation also includes some rather more obscure things, such as motion and rest, and the face of the whole universe. What these things are, and how they might be related to substance in a way like the way you and I and the desk in my office are, are puzzles of the first order.

Again, the denotation of the very term "substance" itself is unclear. It is commonly taken to denote the whole of Nature, the totality of things. But common as this assumption is, there is little in Spinoza's work to justify it, and a good deal to support the contrary assertion that "substance" denotes, not the whole of Nature, but only its active part—those "primary elements of the whole of Nature" which Spinoza describes in the *Treatise on the Correction of the Understanding* as "the source and origin of nature." What, I asked, might these primary elements be?

These deficiencies can now be made good. The term "mode" is to be understood as denoting certain sorts of fact, not individual things. Finite modes are singular facts. The infinite modes are derivative, nomological, general facts, those to which the lower level generalizations in a unified science would correspond. And the primary elements of the whole of Nature, which constitute substance or its attributes, are that set of basic, nomological general facts to which would correspond the highest level generalizations in such a science.

The relation of causal dependence that modes bear to substance is the ontological counterpart of the relation of logical dependence which would obtain between the corresponding propositions in a complete and accurate description of the world. Substance is causally independent of all other entities because it is that set of facts to which the axioms of our unified science correspond. These propositions are not the logical consequence of any others. All other propositions are, in one way or another, logical consequences of them. The derivative nomological propositions follow logically from the axioms, without any other proposition being necessary for their derivation. The facts to which they correspond, the infinite modes, thus depend on the absolute nature of the attributes of substance. The singular propositions follow from the nomological ones—ultimately, that is, from the axioms—but only with the aid of other singular propositions. The facts to which they correspond, the finite modes, thus depend not on the absolute nature of the attributes alone, but also on other finite modes.

The notion of causal dependence which I am employing here is bound to be somewhat unfamiliar. Let me try, briefly, to put it in historical context. In the *Tractatus*, Wittgenstein denied that there are any causal relations. Atomic facts are independent of one another (2.061); from the existence or nonexistence of one atomic fact we cannot infer the existence or nonexistence of another (2.062, cf. 5.134, 5.135). But atomic facts are all the facts there are (cf. 2). As a result, any one fact can either be the case or not be the case, and everything else remains the same (1.21). There is no causal nexus which would justify an inference from the existence of one fact to the existence of another (cf. 5.136). Belief in a causal nexus is superstition (5.1361). A necessity for one thing to happen because another has happened does not exist; there is only logical necessity (6.37).

To interpret Wittgenstein on any matter is perilous, but I take it that in such aphorisms as these we have a genuine denial of causality. The reason for this denial appears to be that Wittgenstein makes two assumptions: (1) it is a necessary condition of one fact's causing another that the proposition describing the cause entail the proposition describing the effect; (2) all the propositions in a complete description of the world would be logically independent of one another, for the world is the totality of atomic facts. If the second assumption is true, then the necessary condition of causality can never be satisfied.

The similarity of this view to Hume's is striking and Wittgenstein clearly has Hume in mind. But I think it would be wrong to say that Hume rejected causality. Rather he presents a reductive analysis of causality, defining "cause" in such a way that it is a necessary condition of one thing's causing another only that the cause precede the effect in time and that the cause be the sort of thing which is regularly followed by things of the kind to which the effect belongs. If I say (to adapt Mark Twain's example) that the man's decision to carry the cat home by the tail caused him some discomfort, I mean that the decision was followed by discomfort and that decisions of this sort generally are. Hume rejects Wittgenstein's first assumption, though not his second. As a result, even though he denies necessary connections,[5] he does not deny causality. Wittgenstein *seems,* at any rate, to want to take this further step.

It is a curious fact of contemporary history that most philosophers in our century have sided with Russell in rejecting Wittgenstein's attempt to reduce general propositions to truth-functions of singular ones, but have tended to accept, with some misgivings, Hume's reduction of causality to regular sequence. Curious, because unnecessary. For if we have both singular facts and general facts at our disposal, we can locate among the furniture of the universe entities whose existence will "entail" the existence of other entities.[6]

The conception of causality which I attribute to Spinoza is unusual at least in the sense that it is not a reductive Humean one. Spinoza accepts Wittgenstein's first assumption, though not his second. Spinoza's conception of causality is also more general in that it does not restrict the causal relation to events (or rather singular facts). We may also speak of causal relationships holding between general facts where the notion of a temporal sequence has no application. And this seems to me quite in order. For surely one of the most important and interesting features of science is that it seeks explanations, not only for individual facts and sequences of facts, but also for the regularities which those individual facts and sequences of facts exemplify. This is one reason for preferring an ontology of facts to one of events.

## Objections and Replies

Such, in outline, is the interpretation of the concepts of substance and mode in Spinoza which I am proposing. It has the advantage of being a fairly definite interpretation. It has, also, the advantage of presenting Spinoza's metaphysic as one which, in my judgment, is coherent and plausible. And it has the advantage, as I have been at pains to point out along the way, of rendering intelligible many things which are otherwise very obscure. But as any interpretation must, it has its disadvantages as well, and it is now time to take some account of the objections that might be raised against it.

One difficulty is that, although this way of taking Spinoza may make sense of a great many passages in his work, it will not deal equally well with all of them. For example, when Spinoza is arguing that substance, as such, is indivisible (*E* Ip12, Ip13, Ip15s), he appears to be thinking of substance in a way far more Cartesian than I have been willing to allow. And though there may not be anything in the passages mentioned which is flatly inconsistent with my interpretation, it is not easy to see how they could be treated in my terms.

This is true, and in reply I can only point out that the adequacy of any interpretation must always be a matter of degree. I feel that my way of reading Spinoza does greater justice to his system as a whole than any other I have seen. But admittedly it falls short of the ideal, which would be to translate each of Spinoza's metaphysical doctrines into its terms.

Another objection, which must inevitably arise, is that I have provided, not an interpretation, but an anachronistic reinterpretation in the light of subsequent thought, of the sort Iris Murdoch was complaining of when she wrote: "there has been of late something of a tendency to read back into the great metaphysicians our own logical formulae, and to treat them as if they were trying ineptly to do what we have done successfully."[7] Just as Joachim saw Spinoza through lenses ground by Hegel and Bradley, so I have seen him through those ground by Russell, Moore, and Wittgenstein.

This is a charge to which I must concede substantial merit. No doubt my preference for translating Spinoza's language into the language of logical atomism is due, in part at least, to my philosophical upbringing. But aside from pointing out how strikingly much of Spinoza can survive the translation—and I am not through yet—there are a number of things to be said in my defense.

First, the seventeenth century is not, after all, such a very remote ancestor of our own century. In many ways it set the problems that have dominated philosophy—or at least English-language philosophy—since then: problems about our knowledge of the external world, about the relations of mind and body, about the nature of space and time and so on. In particular, it gave prominence to the idea that laws play an essential role in explanation. Even if this did not occur in Spinoza, we should have to recognize it in Descartes (cf. the *Principles,* part II). Moreover, we ought not to underestimate the intelligence of these men by supposing that, because they lacked the means we have for expressing ourselves, they could not see what we see. I have attributed to Spinoza the insight that laws alone are not sufficient for the explanation of any particular fact. It does not strike me as implausible that an intelligent man, well-acquainted with the science of his time,[8] should see this. And I take comfort in the fact that some interpreters of Descartes have found it necessary to credit *him* with precisely the same insight.[9]

Again, to some extent we can divorce what I say from how I say it. The conclusion that singular facts do not depend on nomological facts alone can be translated back into Spinoza's language by saying that God is not, insofar as he is infinite, the adequate cause of finite modes, or that what is finite and has a determinate existence does not follow from the *absolute* nature of any attribute of God. This conclusion is an important one. Though it follows from my interpretation of the definitions of substance and mode, it is also supported by considerable textual evidence. It is a conclusion which has been anticipated, but not argued for in detail, by other writers on Spinoza, who have had backgrounds quite different from mine.[10] And it should, I think, survive, whatever view may be taken about the interpretation from which it follows, though I hasten to add that we should like not only to support it textually, but also to have a rationale for it.

Finally, for those of us to whom the metaphysical categories of logical atomism are more perspicuous than those of the seventeenth century, this interpretation can have a certain heuristic value. It can enable us to see relationships between various Spinozistic propositions which we should not otherwise have seen. Had I not first undertaken this exercise in translation, I doubt very much that I should have reached the conclusions I have about the problem of time and eternity in Spinoza, though I am now convinced of the correctness of those conclusions on independent grounds.

Another, more general, and perhaps more important objection is that the interpretation I propose is clearly a naturalistic one, and that it faces the objection which any naturalistic interpretation must face, namely that it does not do justice to what may be called the religious or mystical side of Spinoza.

In order to fix our minds on this problem in a relatively concrete form, we may consider how it has been posed most recently. Paul Seligman, in a very instructive article, has challenged "anyone who is satisfied with an exclusively naturalistic interpretation . . . to ask himself why Spinoza should have felt any need at all of calling his infinite substance *God,* and why he defined God as substance consisting of *infinite* attributes."[11] Now these are certainly both quite pertinent questions. I think we may profitably defer consideration of the second until after we have given some thought to the relation between the attributes, but we have reached a point at which we can say something about the first.

In asking why Spinoza called his one substance "God," we should remember that in the history of Western thought there are at least two gods: the God of Abraham, Isaac, and Jacob, and the God of Plato, Aristotle, and Plotinus—the God of the Old Testament and the God of the Greek philosophers. The first God is conceived as an arbitrary human despot, with his powers and his capriciousness magnified to infinity; the second, as a principle of explanation, an uncaused first cause, embodying a perfection which no finite object can approach. The God of the New Testament, and of Judaeo-Christian theologians since the New Testament, is generally an unhappy compromise between these two.

I submit that Spinoza called his one substance "God" for the perfectly good reason that it had much in common with the God of the philosophers. That it had little in common with the God of the Old Testament could hardly have mattered to him. The aim of Scripture, on his view, is not to present metaphysical truth, but to inculcate morality. To that end it must accommodate itself to the understanding of the people for whom it is intended. There is as much justification for calling the one substance "God" as there is for dignifying with that name the being to whom Luther offered up his prayers—and as little.

To this the reader may reply that there is one feature of crucial importance both in the traditional philosophical conception of God and in Spinoza's conception of his one substance, which I have so far failed to account for, namely, necessary existence. My basic nomological facts may be appropriately described as an uncaused first cause, provided that we understand "first" logically rather than temporally, and they may be "present throughout all of time and space." But, it will be argued, that in no way justifies characterizing them as necessary existents. Unless they can be so characterized, Spinoza's substance will turn out to be merely sempiternal, not eternal, and its identification even with the God of the philosophers will fail. The basic nomological facts are mere brute facts, contingencies for which there is and can be no explanation. And therefore they cannot serve to give an ultimate explanation of the existence of any finite being. Moreover, by limiting God's power as I have, by talking of antecedent conditions stretching back into the infinite past, I have introduced a further element of contingency into the system. But Spinoza's rigorous determinism can no more admit contingency than the traditional philosophic conception of God can admit a limitation on God's power.

This is a very cogent and important objection. I shall do my best to meet it in the next chapter.

Spinoza begins and ends with theological terms; and yet, when we translate his doctrines into modern language, we find a view of the world standing wholly apart from those which have been propounded or seriously influenced by theology. His earlier writings help us to understand the seeming riddle. He started with the intention of making theology philosophical, but with the determination to follow reason to the uttermost. Reason led him beyond the atmosphere of theology altogether, but his advance was so continuous that the full extent of it was hardly perceived by himself.

—Pollock

# 3   Necessity

# Every Truth Is a Necessary Truth

No one who has even the slightest acquaintance with the *Ethics* will
deny that Spinoza's system is rigorously deterministic. That in nature
nothing is contingent, all things being determined by the necessity of
the divine nature to exist and act in a fixed way (*E* Ip29), that things
could have been produced by God in no other way and in no other
order than they have been (*E* Ip33), are among the best known and
most important propositions in that work. But to ascertain their precise
meaning is a task more difficult than might at first appear.

We may seek to capture their import in a manner congenial to modern
ears by various paraphrases. We may say, with Hampshire, that for
Spinoza the actual world is the only possible world (p. 42), or with
C. de Deugd, that all possibility is actuality to an omniscient being
(p. 70). Or we may say, as I should prefer to, that for Spinoza every
truth is a necessary truth. But each of these formulas will be found
to harbor ambiguities, and it is no easy matter to decide which interpretation of them comes closest to expressing Spinoza's intent.

Let us take the last one first. One of the theses I wish to defend
in this chapter is that although Spinoza is committed to the view that
every truth is a necessary truth, he is also committed, quite consistently,
to the view that some are not. This, however, is a needlessly paradoxical
way of putting it. To remove the air of contradiction, we need to make
a distinction: all truths are necessary, but not all truths are necessary
in the same sense; some are necessary in a sense which allows, indeed
which requires, that in another equally legitimate sense they are not
necessary but contingent.

Still, before exploring the senses of "necessary" involved here, it will
be best to first consider the thesis that every truth is a necessary one
as naïvely as we can, without raising any question as to its possible
meanings.

Prima facie, there would seem to be very strong objections to the
thesis. For one thing, there are many propositions which we should

wish to call true, but which we should not wish to call necessarily true, on the ground that, for all we can tell, they could have been false. It is true that Spinoza had dark hair, but that truth does not strike us as a necessary one. To use a test of necessary truth made popular by Hume, its falsity is conceivable; to suppose that Spinoza did not have dark hair does not appear to involve us in any contradiction.

Moreover, it is natural to wonder what sort of justification Spinoza could possibly give for saying that a proposition like "Spinoza had dark hair" is necessarily true. If Spinoza had been Leibniz and held a Leibnizian view of individual concepts, then we might be able to construct a justification. According to Leibniz,[1] all true propositions about individuals—except existential ones—are in principle capable of being shown to be identities, that is, of the form "*A* is *A*" or "*AB* is *A*." The reason for this is that the concept of an individual is supposed by him to include the concept of every predicate that may be truly ascribed to the individual at any time in his life, except the predicate ". . . exists." Hence, on Leibniz' view of individual concepts, any true nonexistential proposition about Spinoza would be, or would seem to be, what we should call today an analytic truth.[2] Just as we might show "all bachelors are unmarried" to be analytically true by substituting for the subject term, "bachelor," its definition, "unmarried male," so we could show "Spinoza had dark hair" to be analytically true by substituting for "Spinoza" his definition or individual concept. Presumably the correct account of "Spinoza had dark hair," in Leibnizian terms, would be something like this:

> The individual who was born in Amsterdam, on 24 November 1632, to Michael and Hannah Spinoza . . . was educated under Rabbi Saul Morteira and Rabbi Manasseh ben Israel . . . had dark hair . . . wrote the *Ethics* . . . ground lenses for a living . . . and died at the Hague, on 21 February 1677, had dark hair.

Since this has at least the appearance of being analytically true, and since few philosophers would question the necessity of analytic truths,

a Leibnizian account would give Spinoza some sort of justification for
holding the proposition "Spinoza had dark hair," and others like it,
to be necessarily true.

There would be some difficulty about this. First, and obviously, reference to other individuals has been made in spelling out the individual
concept of Spinoza. Since each of these, in turn, has an individual concept capable of analysis, the account presented here could not be an
ultimate one even if we were able to fill in all the blanks. Giving a
complete analysis of a singular proposition is going to be difficult at
best. Leibniz holds that it requires going through an infinite process
and is possible only for God. Statements involving essential reference
to individuals may thus be characterized as infinitely analytic. By contrast,
those dealing with abstractions, such as "The wise man is happy," are
finitely analytic. A full analysis of the concept of the subject is possible
without going through an infinite process, and consequently the reduction to an identity can be accomplished by man.

But second, and not so obviously, the analysis of the concept of an
individual involves a regress which is not merely infinite, but viciously
so.[3] Suppose we set out to give an analysis of the concept of Spinoza
along the lines suggested above. At some stage we shall wish to replace
the proper name "Manasseh ben Israel" by a definite description which
gives its analysis. If that analysis is to be complete, then the definite
description will have the form "The individual who was born in Lisbon
in 1604 . . . was Rabbi of the second Amsterdam Synagogue . . .
educated Spinoza . . . went to England on a mission to Oliver Crom-
well . . ." and so on through a complete enumeration of Manasseh's
properties. But that will not be enough. We shall also have to replace
all the proper names in this definite description by definite descriptions
of their own—and among them, of course, is the name "Spinoza." In
short, we cannot give a complete analysis of the individual concept of
Spinoza until we have a complete analysis of the individual concept
of Manasseh ben Israel; but we cannot give a complete analysis of
the concept of Manasseh ben Israel unless we already have at hand
a complete analysis of the concept of Spinoza. Under these circum-

stances, even God might find it hard to give a complete analysis of the concept of an individual.

Still, whatever difficulties there might be in a Leibnizian account of singular propositions, if Spinoza had held views like those of Leibniz, then we might be able to understand his thinking that every truth is a necessary truth. But Spinoza manifestly did not hold such views.

First of all, Leibniz' doctrine of individual concepts, as he himself points out, involves him in bringing back the substantial forms of the medieval philosophers. But substantial forms were very much out of fashion in Leibniz' time, and no one rejected them more emphatically than Spinoza (*Ep.* 56, IV:261–262). Again, Leibniz inferred from his doctrine of individual concepts that every individual substance was a world apart, dependent on and affected by no other substance but God. Had Spinoza held the same doctrine, he would have inferred similarly that men are always active, never passive (*E* III D1–3), and consequently that they are always virtuous and free (*E* IVP18s). That he could not have accepted such a conclusion is too obvious to need proof. So the Leibnizian route can provide no explanation for Spinoza's holding that every truth is a necessary one.

## In What Sense Every Truth Is a Necessary Truth

To understand how Spinoza might try to justify his doctrine that every truth is necessarily so, we shall need to consider what sort of analysis Spinoza suggests for the concept of necessary truth. We shall find it to be different in important respects from that of Leibniz. According to the latter, true propositions divide into truths of reason (necessary truths) and truths of fact (contingent ones). Truths of reason are true in virtue of the principle of contradiction: their denials involve a contradiction, either explicitly or implicitly. Examples would be the proposition that God exists and the laws of logic and mathematics.

Truths of fact are true in virtue of the principle of sufficient reason, which says, on one version at least,[4] that nothing happens without a reason why it should be so rather than otherwise. Examples would be existential propositions (except the proposition that God exists), the laws of nature, and singular propositions.

Since singular propositions are reducible through definitions to identities, it might appear that they ought to be classed as truths of reason rather than as truths of fact. But Leibniz resists this conclusion. Sometimes his ground for denying that they are strictly necessary seems to be that they are infinitely rather than finitely analytic, though this seems inadequate. It suggests that the contingency of these propositions is an illusion of the finite intellect. Sometimes, more plausibly, his ground seems to be that, although all nonexistential propositions about individuals are analytic, existential ones are not. "Spinoza had dark hair," if true, is analytically true; but it is not necessarily true without qualification, for it is true only if "Spinoza exists" is true. This latter proposition is not necessary, but contingent, as it depends on God's free decision to create this world, a decision motivated but not necessitated by the fact that this world, if created, would be the best of all possible worlds.

If I am correct in giving (1) "The individual who . . . had dark hair . . . had dark hair" as the proper Leibnizian account of (2) "Spinoza had dark hair," then I suppose most contemporary philosophers would agree with Leibniz that (1), despite its appearance of analyticity, is not necessarily true. On a Russellian account of definite descriptions (1) is false if there is no such individual. On a Strawsonian account it is neither true nor false.[5]

Leibniz will allow that truths of fact are necessary in one possible sense of the term. Though they may fail to be true and are therefore not absolutely necessary, nevertheless they are hypothetically necessary. Given God's decision to create this world, rather than some other possible world, things could not have been otherwise. But God need not have so decided. His decision had a cause in his knowledge that this world would be the best of all possible worlds, and it could have been predicted with certainty, but it was not absolutely necessary. And therefore, neither is the world which follows from it.

The similarities and differences between Leibniz and Spinoza on this point are instructive. Consider, for example, the following passage in the *Ethics:*

> Since I have shown by the preceding, more clearly than by noon light, that there is absolutely nothing in things on account of which they may be called contingent, I wish now to explain briefly what we must understand by contingent; but first, necessary and impossible.
>
> A thing is called necessary either by reason of its essence or by reason of its cause. For the existence of any thing follows necessarily either from its essence and definition, or from a given efficient cause.
>
> For the same reasons are things said to be impossible, that is, either because the essence or definition of the thing involves a contradiction, or because there is no external cause determinate for the production of such a thing.
>
> But a thing is not called contingent except on account of a defect in our knowledge. For if we do not know that the thing's essence involves a contradiction, or if, knowing that it involves no contradiction, we nevertheless can affirm nothing with certainty about its existence, because the order of causes is hidden from us, then the thing can never appear either necessary or impossible to us. And hence we call it either contingent or possible. (*E* Ip33s)

Now Spinoza is talking here about the necessity or impossibility of things, rather than of truths, and he speaks only of the necessity or impossibility of the existence of things, and not of the necessity or impossibility of their possessing certain properties or entering into certain relations. But this need not prevent us from translating what he says about things into talk about truths and developing a general account of necessary truth that will accord with Spinoza's intentions.

It might be objected at this point that to interpret Spinoza in this

way presupposes that he did not have the vocabulary to talk about
necessary truths instead of necessary things. But this distinction and vocabulary were, it might be argued, available to him. If he did not use
them, it was either from carelessness, which seems unlikely, or by
intention.

Quite so. The vocabulary was available and Spinoza deliberately
avoided using it. His reasons for avoiding it are of some interest. In
a letter to Simon de Vries (*Ep.* 10), Spinoza writes:

> You ask whether things or the affections of things are also eternal
> truths? I say, certainly. If you ask why I do not call them eternal
> truths, I reply: to distinguish them, as everyone customarily does,
> from those things which do not explain any thing or any affection
> of a thing. For example, nothing comes into existence from nothing.
> This, I say, and similar propositions are called absolutely eternal
> truths, by which men wish to signify only that such things have
> no place outside the mind.

I take it that Spinoza avoided talk of necessary truths because he wanted
it to be clear that he was talking about the world, about something
that had existence *extra mentem*. Lacking the convenient term "fact"
to serve as an ontological correlate of the term "truth," he had to make
do with the inconvenient term "thing."

But though the ontological import of Spinoza's doctrine must always
be kept in mind, I think we can most easily come to terms with Spinoza
if we represent him as holding the following view. All propositions are
either necessarily true or necessarily false. This will hold both for existential and for nonexistential propositions. But, restricting ourselves to
truths, not all truths are necessary in the same sense. Some are absolutely
necessary, in the Leibnizian sense that their denial is explicitly or implicitly self-contradictory: their truth follows from the essence or definition of the subject. But others are only relatively necessary. Their denial
does not involve a contradiction, either explicitly or implicitly. Their

truth, rather, is grounded in the fact that they follow logically from other propositions which are true, propositions which given an efficient causal explanation of them.

Relative necessity is like Leibniz' hypothetical necessity. It has the form: given $p$, $q$ is necessary. But it is also, and more important, unlike hypothetical necessity. The proposition (or set of propositions) relative to which $q$ is necessary provides an explanation in terms of efficient causation. Leibniz' hypothetically necessary propositions are explained, ultimately, in terms of a final cause, God's decision to create the best of all possible worlds.

Again, Leibniz' hypothetically necessary propositions do have an ultimate ground in the will of God. Spinoza's relatively necessary propositions are grounded both in the will, or intellect, of God (the laws of nature) and in an infinite series of prior finite causes. Hence, in a sense they have no ultimate cause.

Finally, and most important, Leibniz' hypothetically necessary propositions are ultimately grounded in something which is itself supposed to be contingent. Assuming a good argument for the contingency of God's will, Leibniz is right to describe his hypothetically necessary propositions as in themselves contingent. But a relatively necessary proposition in Spinoza's system is grounded in a series of other propositions each of which is either absolutely or relatively necessary. Therefore, though it would be correct to say that they are contingent in the sense of not being absolutely necessary, this would be misleading, as it might suggest the Leibnizian picture of things.

Since some may find this conclusion difficult to accept, let me adduce one further passage in support of it. Consider the case of true propositions of the form "$x$ exists" where the values of the variable $x$ are singular referring expressions for example, "God," "Spinoza," "this table," etc. It is clear that, like Leibniz, Spinoza would say that only one such proposition is absolutely necessary, namely, "God exists."[6] Otherwise he would not say that "The essence of things produced by God does not involve existence" (*E* Ip24). But for Spinoza, this does not preclude saying that true existential propositions are necessary in some other sense. Witness the following passage:

> For each thing there must be assigned a cause or reason why it exists or why it does not exist. For example, if a triangle exists, there must be a reason or cause why it exists; and if it does not exist, there must also be a reason or cause which prevents or denies its existence.
>
> This reason or cause must be contained either in the nature of the thing or outside it. For example, its own nature proclaims the reason why a square circle does not exist, because it involves a contradiction. The reason why substance, on the other hand, exists, also follows from its nature alone, because it involves existence (P7).
>
> But the reason why a circle or a triangle exists or does not exist does not follow from the nature of these things, but from the order of corporeal nature as a whole. For from this it must follow, either that a triangle does *now* exist, or that it does not *now* exist.
> (*E* IP11D2, my italics)

Those things whose reason for existence is contained in their nature are clearly the things called necessary by reason of their essence in *E* IP33S. To say that the reason for a thing's existence is contained in its nature is equivalent to saying that the proposition asserting its existence is absolutely necessary. We may wish to say that there is only one such thing existing, namely substance. Or we may wish to say that there are many, namely all the attributes of substance. For substance simply *is* the sum of its attributes. But whichever we say, substance, or all of the attributes of substance, are eternal (*E* IP20). It would be misleading, though correct, to say that they exist now, since this would suggest that the nonexistence of the attributes at some other time is a logical possibility, which it is not.

But to say that the reason of a thing lies outside its nature, in the

order of corporeal nature as a whole (*E* Ip11), or in the given efficient
cause (*E* Ip33s), is equivalent to saying that the proposition asserting
its existence is not absolutely, but only relatively necessary. This will
be true of the modes of substance generally (with the possible, but awk-
ward exception of the infinite modes). Since, for any mode now existing,
its nonexistence at some other time is logically possible, there is no inap-
propriateness in saying that it now exists. And Spinoza does speak in
this way of the modes.

On this interpretation, Spinoza can offer either of two explanations
for the apparent contingency of some true propositions. Either we do
not know the essence of the thing sufficiently clearly to perceive the
absolute necessity of the proposition, or we lack sufficient scientific information to perceive its relative necessity. This lack of information may
be an ignorance of the relevant laws, or of the antecedent conditions,
or both. The reason why an omniscient being cannot feign anything,
in the sense of supposing something to be the case which is not, is that
neither the order of essences nor the order of causes is concealed from
him. Relative to his perfect knowledge of the definitions of things,
of the laws of nature, and of the antecedent conditions, the hypothesis
that Spinoza did not have dark hair would possess the same kind of
impossibility for him which the hypothesis that there is a round square
possesses for us.[7]

For Leibniz, on the other hand, all and only absolutely necessary
propositions are necessary. Hence, he gives only the first of Spinoza's
two alternatives as an explanation of the apparent contingency of some
necessary propositions: that we do not have adequate knowledge of the
essence of the thing.

With regard to truths which are not absolutely necessary, he will
say that we sometimes fail to perceive their reason, or cause, but not
that we fail to perceive their necessity. For they are not, strictly speaking,
necessary. The explanation for our failure to perceive their reason will
be, not that we do not know the efficient causal explanation of the
facts but that we do not know their explanation in terms of final causes.

We do not see how the existence of this or that state of affairs serves to realize some value.

## Why Every Truth Is a Necessary Truth

So far I have been concerned to show that Spinoza's universal denial of contingency is compatible with the admission that some truths are contingent, in one important sense of that ambiguous term. His determinism has the form:

(1) Every truth is either absolutely or relatively necessary,
and not the form:

(2) Every truth is absolutely necessary.
Now I want to consider the problem of how Spinoza might justify this claim. I think that if we grant Spinoza certain assumptions, assumptions which I am confident that he would make, his thesis must be true. So let me list those assumptions, and consider briefly the grounds he has for them.

(1) The proposition that God exists is absolutely necessary.

(2) All other singular truths, though absolutely contingent, have a scientific explanation, in the sense that they follow from a statement of certain antecedent conditions and nomological propositions. Hence they are relatively necessary.

(3) All accidental general truths, though absolutely contingent, have a scientific explanation in the same sense, and hence are also relatively necessary.

(4) All nomological general truths are absolutely necessary.
These four theses assign each of four classes of truth to one or the other of the two categories of necessary truth. If the classification is exhaustive, as it seems to be, and if each thesis is true, then Spinoza's determinism is established. So we may proceed to ask whether Spinoza would make these claims and how he would support them.

That he would make the first is certain. It is $E$ Ip11. And the various proofs adduced for that proposition make clear that it is absolute necessity which is being attributed to God. The argument is fundamentally the familiar ontological one, though, as I have suggested above, it takes an unfamiliar form in Spinoza because of his unusual conception of God.

That he would make the second is also, I think, tolerably certain from *E* Ip28 and from the discussion of miracles in the *Theological-Political Treatise*. But it requires the long argument of Chapter 2 to see it, and I shall not repeat that argument here. His assertion of (2) is based partly on confidence in the competence of science to handle all questions of explanation and partly on theological-philosophical considerations springing from his identification of God with Nature:

> As for the first [that nothing happens contrary to nature, but that she observes an eternal order, fixed and immutable], this is easily shown from what we have demonstrated in Chapter IV about the divine law: namely, that whatever God wishes or determines involves eternal necessity and truth. For we showed from the fact that God's intellect is not distinguished from his will, that we affirm the same thing, whether we say that God wills something, or that he understands it. So by the same necessity with which it follows from the nature and perfection of God that he understands each thing as it is, it also follows that he wills each thing as it is. Moreover, since nothing is necessarily true except by divine decree alone, it follows most clearly that the universal laws of nature are mere decrees of God which follow from the necessity and perfection of the divine nature. If, therefore, anything were to happen in nature inconsistent with her universal laws, it would also necessarily be inconsistent with the decree, intellect, and nature of God. (*TTP* vi, III:82–83)

Spinoza is arguing here from the perfection of God and from his characteristic theological doctrine that in God will and intellect are identical. I shall have more to say about this later.

A less theologically oriented passage occurs later in the chapter, when Spinoza is arguing, in effect, that reason must be the judge of what is truly scriptural:

> Wherefore we may here conclude absolutely that whatever is truly narrated in Scripture as having happened must have happened, like all things, according to the laws of nature. And if anything is found which can be demonstrated in a clear proof either to be inconsistent with the laws of nature, or to have been unable to follow logically from them, surely we must believe that it has been added to the Sacred Writings by sacreligious men. For whatever is contrary to nature is contrary to reason, and what is contrary to reason is absurd, and accordingly to be rejected. (*TTP* vi, III:91)

Here he seems to be taking the view that for a singular truth not to have a scientific explanation would involve a contradiction.

The third thesis—that all accidental general truths are relatively necessary—is not so easy to document. My reason for attributing it to Spinoza lies in *E* Ip8s2. There Spinoza, in the course of arguing that there can only be one substance of the same nature, has occasion to discuss the proposition that there exist exactly twenty men, which Spinoza supposes for the sake of the discussion to be true. Spinoza contends that:

> If a certain number of individuals exist in nature, there must necessarily be a cause why those individuals, and neither more nor fewer, exist. For example, if there are twenty men in existence . . . it will not be sufficient in order to provide a reason why twenty men exist to show the cause of human nature in general. It will be necessary as well to show the cause why neither more nor fewer than twenty exist. But this cause cannot be contained in human nature itself, since the true definition of man does not involve the number twenty. Therefore the cause why these twenty men exist, and consequently why each exists, must be outside each. (II:50–51)

Spinoza goes on to conclude that wherever a thing is of a kind which can have several individuals it must have an external cause. Since it pertains to the nature of substance to exist (that is, it does not have an external cause), there can only be one substance of the same kind.

The thing that is interesting about this passage for our purposes, however, is that the proposition "There are [exactly] twenty men" would be an example of an "accidental" generalization and that Spinoza seems to want to assimilate this proposition to singular propositions and to say that it is necessary in precisely the same way they are. This is why I suggested in the preceding chapter that we might try to understand Spinoza in terms of the (Popperian) view that accidental generalizations are equivalent to singular propositions or truth-functions of singular propositions.[8]

This is a view to which there are, of course, familiar objections. It is commonly held that no set of singular propositions ever entails a general proposition. Suppose that Brown, Jones, and Smith are the only men in the tearoom at 4:00 and that Brown, Jones, and Smith are wearing shoes. From the premises that

Brown is in the tearoom at 4:00 and Brown is wearing shoes.
Jones is in the tearoom at 4:00 and Jones is wearing shoes.
Smith is in the tearoom at 4:00 and Smith is wearing shoes.

we cannot infer that

All the men in the tearoom at 4:00 are wearing shoes.

unless we have the additional premise that

Brown, Jones, and Smith are all the men in the tearoom at 4:00.

And this is a general proposition. If no set of singular propositions ever entails a general proposition, then general propositions, whether strictly universal or not, cannot be reducible (that is, equivalent) to singular propositions or truth-functions of singular propositions.[9]

This objection is widely regarded as conclusive. One might, however, undertake to rebut it in the following way. Though the additional proposition which is necessary for the derivation of our general conclusion, that is,

Brown, Jones, and Smith are all the men in the tearoom at 4:00

might ordinarily be regarded as a general proposition, nevertheless, if we consider the way it would be established we shall see that this is a mistake. The proposition would be established by examining the room as a whole to see whether or not it is occupied by men other than Brown, Jones, and Smith. The additional premise required, therefore, can be (is properly) regarded as a singular proposition about the room as a whole, to the effect that

The tearoom at 4:00 is entirely free of other men.

This certainly satisfies the usual test for singular propositions: its subject term is a singular referring expression. Moreover, like the typical singular proposition, but unlike the typical universal proposition, it does not need to be established by inference. It can be known by direct observation. For that matter, our original conclusion might have been transformed immediately into a similar proposition about the whole of this particular region of space and time:

The tearoom at 4:00 is entirely free of shoeless men.

or, if our original conclusion is thought to imply that there are men in the room at that time:

The tearoom at 4:00 is not entirely free of men, but it is entirely free of shoeless men.

In general, wherever a universal generalization is restricted to a particular region of space and time, it is equivalent to a singular proposition about the whole of that region.

Whether or not this is a satisfactory rebuttal, I shall not undertake to say here. But it does seem to me to be the sort of thing some logicians might wish to say,[10] and it also seems to me an appropriate way of looking at Spinoza. For by redrawing the usual distinction between universal and singular propositions, it makes the fundamental logical antithesis the contrast between the infinite and the finite. And this, I think, is very much as it should be.

This brings us to the fourth and most interesting claim, that all nomological propositions are absolutely necessary. Here we may appeal to Spinoza's own account of the notion of a law in the *Theological-Political Treatise*. After defining a law generally as "that according to which each individual, or all or some members of the same species, act in one and the same fixed and definite manner," Spinoza goes on to distinguish between two kinds of law, those which depend on natural necessity and those which depend on human conventions:

> A law which depends on natural necessity is one which follows
> necessarily from the nature or definition of the thing, whereas one
> which depends on human convention, and is more properly called
> an ordinance, is one which men prescribe for themselves and others
> in order to live more safely and comfortably, or for some other
> reasons. For example, that all bodies, when they strike other, smaller
> ones, lose as much of their motion as they communicate to the
> others, is a universal law of all bodies, which follows from the
> necessity of nature. Similarly, that a man, when he recalls one
> thing, immediately recalls another like it, or one which he has per-
> ceived simultaneously with it, is a law which follows necessarily
> from human nature. But that men should yield, or be forced to
> yield, something of the right which they have by nature, or that
> they should commit themselves to live in a certain way, these things
> depend on human convention. (*TTP* iv, III:57–58)

Here we find Spinoza making quite clearly the now familiar distinction between descriptive and prescriptive laws. But what is important for our purposes is that Spinoza wishes to regard the laws of nature (though not the laws of men) as possessing the same kind of necessity the proposition "God exists" is supposed by him to possess; they follow necessarily from definitions, and are hence absolutely necessary. Given our identification of the essence of God with the fundamental nomological facts, this is just what we should expect.

The view that nomological propositions are absolutely necessary is not one likely to find much favor among contemporary philosophers. They would argue that the laws of nature must be established empirically—by examining nature, not by drawing out the consequences of definitions. And therefore, they would conclude, scientific laws cannot be absolutely necessary.

What Spinzoa's reply to this objection would have been is hard to determine. But without going very deeply into his theory of knowledge, which deserves a separate and thorough treatment, let me suggest that he might well have rejected the assumption, implicit in this objection, that what is established empirically cannot also be established a priori. It is, after all, implied in his discussion of the Rule of Three that even the necessary truths of mathematics may be arrived at by any one of the three kinds of knowledge.

There was, moreover, much in the science of his time which might have encouraged him to take a similar view of physics. The unprejudiced and attentive reader of Galileo's *Two New Sciences* cannot fail to be struck by the frequency with which that paradigm of the empirical scientist appeals to a priori arguments as well as to a posteriori ones. For instance, when Salviati proposes to define uniformly accelerated motion as that motion which, starting from rest, acquires equal increments of speed in equal intervals of time, however small the time interval, Sagredo raises a doubt as to whether this definition

> corresponds to and describes that kind of accelerated motion which we meet in nature in the case of freely falling bodies,[11]

for if it did,

> then there is no degree of speed however small . . . with which
> we may not find a body travelling after starting from rest . . .
> [but] our senses show us that a heavy falling body suddenly acquires
> a great speed.

Salviati replies first that the experience which seems to show this is
misleading. He next adduces empirical support for his assumption of
a gradual increase of speed, and contends that

> the same experiment which at first glance seemed to show one thing,
> when more carefully examined assures us of the contrary.

And then he concludes with an a priori argument:

> But without depending upon the above experiment, which is doubt-
> less very conclusive, it seems to me that it ought not to be difficult
> to establish such a fact by reasoning alone.

The argument that follows is not a very good one. Neither, for that
matter, is his empirical argument. But the procedure which this passage
illustrates is a common one in Galileo.[12]

The traditional notion of Galileo as the experimental scientist par
excellence has, of late, come under heavy attack from historians of science. Recent research strongly suggests that many of the experiments
he described were never performed. Had they been, they would not
have yielded the right results. But in trusting to reason, or rather to
what we might call, following Bacon, a union of the experimental and
rational faculties, Galileo gave voice to an ideal of science which dominated his age. As the science of nature developed, A. R. Hall writes,

> it became clear that its starting point, the Laws of Motion, from
> which everything else could be derived, with the aid of suitable

definitions, according to mathematical strictness, did not have to rest solely on the dubious validity of such experimental tests as could be devised by men upon the surface of the Earth. It seemed that the Laws of Motion *could not be false,* that is, that it was inconceivable that any alternative propositions could be valid . . . It was superfluous to attempt to test the laws by experiments under conditions that in any case could never correspond to those under which the laws would be rigorously true. Such experiments did not prove the laws, but illustrated their applicability. Accordingly the science of motion did not depend altogether on inference and the accuracy of experiments for its application to those bodies beyond the reach of experiment, unless it should be true that Nature was not everywhere uniform and "conformable to herself"—which no 17th Century philosopher or scientist was prepared to suppose.[13]

This is not to say, of course, that Spinoza was right in thinking the laws of nature to be absolutely necessary. But it does suggest that Spinoza's view was an intelligible one for a seventeenth-century philosopher to hold. In the final section of this chapter, I shall consider whether or not it is an intelligible view for a twentieth-century philosopher to hold.

## Is the Actual World the Only Possible World?

So far I have treated Spinoza's determinism in relation to the thesis that every truth is a necessary one, arguing that, correctly understood, this will serve to express Spinoza's meaning and that, so understood, it permits a kind of contingency to creep into his system. Then I explored the rationale for the thesis. Now I wish to ask whether, on this interpretation, the thesis does entail that the actual world is the only possible world.

Before we can answer that question, however, we must decide what meaning we are to attach to the latter proposition. It is not at all obvious that it has any clear meaning. After Leibniz, we tend to picture an infinite number of possible worlds, of which the actual world is the one that happens, by grace of God or Chance, to exist. To say that the actual world is the only possible world seems to be to say that, of all the infinity of possible worlds, only one is possible. There are possible worlds that are not possible. If the proposition does not say this, then it is not clear what the actual world is being contrasted with.

The difficulty is surmountable. The intent of our formula can be captured if we rephrase it as "of all prima facie possible worlds, only the actual world is really possible." What this means might be explained in the following way. Suppose we conceive, as we have in the preceding chapter, of a complete description of the world, a set of propositions $A$, containing every truth about the past, present, and future. Let us then define a prima facie possible world as the descriptum of any set of propositions which is either identical with $A$ or formed from $A$ by negating one, some, or all of the propositions in $A$, and conjoining these negations with every proposition in $A$ which has not been negated. The actual world will be the descriptum of $A$.

Using a device analogous to a truth table, we might first list the propositions of $A$ horizontally, and then, in vertical columns under each proposition in $A$, list either that proposition or its negation, in the following manner:

1. $p$   $q$   $r$ . . . .
2. $Np$   $q$   $r$ . . . .
3. $p$   $Nq$   $r$ . . . .
4. $Np$   $Nq$   $r$ . . . .
5. $p$   $q$   $Nr$ . . . .
6. $Np$   $q$   $Nr$ . . . .
7. $p$   $Nq$   $Nr$ . . . .
8. $Np$   $Nq$   $Nr$ . . . .

In this way all possible combinations of propositions and their negations will be covered. If $A$ contained only three propositions, $p$, $q$, and $r$, our table would have only three columns and eight rows. There would be only eight prima facie possible worlds. Since $A$ contains infinitely many propositions, the table will extend indefinitely to the right and indefinitely downward.

The claim that the actual world is the only possible world can now be made more clear. It will mean that there is only one row in the table that constitutes a self-consistent set of propositions, namely, the top row. Every other set involves a contradiction.

Given that every truth is either absolutely or relatively necessary, it is easy to see what the grounds for this would have to be. Any proposition in $A$ which is absolutely necessary, say $p$, cannot be consistently denied. Hence any set of propositions containing $Np$ will fail to be self-consistent. This will eliminate many rows on the table. Any proposition in $A$ which is not absolutely necessary, say $q$, will be relatively necessary. That is, $q$ will be entailed by some other proposition $r$ which is also in $A$. So any set containing $Nq$ and $r$ will be inconsistent. And again, many rows will be eliminated.

Clearly, if every truth is either absolutely or relatively necessary, then a great many rows of the table will turn out to be inconsistent. But equally clearly, in the end we will have to admit a plurality of self-consistent rows. For consider the case of our relatively necessary proposition $q$. In itself it is contingent, so no row containing $Nq$ is ruled out on that ground alone. Relative to another proposition $r$, it is necessary, so any row containing $Nq$ and $r$ is impossible. But what of rows containing $Nq$ and $Nr$? The proposition $r$ will be a conjunction of an absolutely necessary proposition, $s$, and a relatively necessary proposition, $t$. The conjunction can be consistently denied if one of its conjuncts, $s$ and $t$, can. The former, being absolutely necessary, cannot. Can the latter? Well, it is only necessary relative to another proposition, $u$. The conjunction of $Nt$ and $u$ is inconsistent, but the conjunction of $Nt$ and $Nu$ may be all right. So the same question arises about $t$ that arose about $q$, and it gets the same answer. We are off and running now on the philosophers' favorite horse, the infinite regress. But this is a very gentle, well-mannered regress. Not vicious at all.

In short, had we but world enough and time, we could form a self-consistent set of propositions by taking any relatively necessary proposition in $A$, negating it, and then negating any other relatively necessary proposition we have to in order to maintain consistency. We will be forced to deny infinitely many relatively necessary propositions, but with patience and perseverance we can still arrive at a complete set, consistent in itself, but inconsistent with $A$. If every truth is necessary, but some are only relatively necessary, then the actual world is not the only possible world. Only if every truth were absolutely necessary would the Leibnizian formula follow.

The result is interesting and, I venture to say, conclusively demonstrated by the preceding argument. Whether or not it would have been acceptable to Spinoza is not so easy to decide. But it is worth pointing out that the Leibnizian formula may be interpreted in other ways, according to which Spinoza *would* be able to say that the actual world is the only possible world.

Suppose we take one of the other rows in the table which gives a self-consistent set of propositions and describes another prima facie possible world that is really possible, though not actual. Call the set $B$ and the world it describes the $B$-world. Can it exist? In a sense, of course, it can. It is, as C. I. Lewis might say, a consistently thinkable world. But in another sense, it cannot, merely because the $A$-world exists and the existence of the $B$-world is incompatible with the existence of the $A$-world. To say that both of these worlds existed would be to say that a proposition and its negation might both be true. In this sense, perhaps a trivial one, the actual world is the only possible world. Given the way the term "world" is being used here, there could not be more than one prima facie possible world which was actual.

This would appear to be the sort of situation ruled out by $E$ Ip5: "there cannot be two or more substances having the same nature." If the worlds described by $A$ and $B$ both existed, there would be two substances having the same nature. They would have the same nature, because $B$ must contain exactly the same nomological propositions as

*A*. Otherwise, since the nomological propositions are absolutely necessary, it would not be a self-consistent set. So the *B*-world must be distinguished from the *A*-world only by a difference in its modifications, in that *B* would contain different nonnomological propositions. In saying that these two worlds cannot coexist, we are saying that Spinoza is right to hold that there cannot be two or more substances having the same nature.

This line of thought can be pushed a bit further. We can argue not only that there cannot be two substances having the same nature, but also that there cannot be two substances having different natures. If the *B*-world has a different nature than the *A*-world, then it will contain the negation of one or more of *A*'s nomological propositions. But the nomological propositions are absolutely necessary. So the *B*-world simply could not exist. There could not be a world, or substance, having a nature different from that of the actual world. And since we have already argued that there could not be another substance of the same nature, there could not be two or more substances, period. Such is the rationale we might give, on this interpretation, for that fundamental theorem of the *Ethics* which says that "Besides God, no substance can be or be conceived" (Ip14).

If there is some other self-consistent row, the world described by that set of propositions cannot exist in addition to the world described by *A*. In that sense, surely, the actual world is the only possible world. But perhaps Spinoza would wish to hold that the actual world is the only possible world in the stronger sense that the actual world, in all its detail, must exist. If the *B*-world is really possible, though not actual, it seems a fair question to ask Spinoza "Why not?" It hardly seems sufficient to say that it can't because the *A*-world does. What we mean is "Why the *A*-world rather than the *B*-world?" If Spinoza is going to rule this question out of order, then he is going to accept a limitation on the principle of sufficient reason. He is going to admit that there is something whose existence is without a reason or cause. He cannot answer that the *A*-world exists because its existence is logically necessary given the necessary truth of its nomological propositions. The *B*-world possesses exactly the same reason for existence, since *B* contains exactly the same nomological propositions. If it were not for a difference in the nonnomological propositions they contain, *A* would be identical with *B*. Our question is this: "Why do the nomological propositions, whose absolute necessity we are conceding for the sake of argument, have the instances they have, rather than some other possible set of instances?" It may be that Spinoza would reject the question. It certainly seems that he should. But if we say that he would, we must remember that our ground for this is merely that he has to, to be consistent with his account of necessity. We should remember also that it seems to entail a qualification on the principle of sufficient reason that Spinoza never explicitly makes.

Still, even if Spinoza does not, on the most natural interpretation, hold the actual world to be the only possible world, his determinism is quite strong enough to be philosophically interesting. Any given event is to be seen as the necessary outcome of prior events. Certainly this form of determinism raises all the familiar problems about moral responsibility.

## Objections and Replies Again

At the end of the last chapter I posed two questions. First, have I not, by my talk of antecedent conditions stretching back into the infinite past, introduced an alien element of contingency into the system? Second, are not the basic nomological facts contingent, and hence merely sempiternal, or is there some basis for holding them to be necessary and eternal? To the first of these questions I answer, firmly, yes and no. There is, on my interpretation, an element of contingency in the system. How far it is an alien element introduced into the system I cannot say. There certainly are substantial grounds for thinking that it is not.

To turn now to the second question, it would appear that it has already been answered in dealing with the first question. For Spinoza the basic nomological propositions, indeed, all nomological propositions, and consequently the facts they describe, are logically necessary in the most strict and absolute sense. But this answer is the source of much difficulty, both for the internal consistency of the system and for its plausibility.

In the first place, if all nomological propositions are absolutely necessary, then the infinite modes, the facts described by the derivative nomological propositions, possess the same reason for existence that substance does. Their essence, to use Spinoza's terminology, involves existence, and they are their own cause (*E* ID1), independent of everything else. This is implied in Spinoza's description of them as infinite and eternal, for eternity, by definition, involves necessary existence and not just existence without beginning or end (*E* ID8). But this conflicts with the description of them as modes. A mode, by definition, is an effect, something dependent in nature, something whose existence is not self-explanatory. An eternal mode is a contradiction in terms.

This difficulty does not arise merely because of my somewhat idiosyncratic way of interpreting Spinoza. It has been noted and dealt with by Wolfson, who argues that Spinoza simply does not mean what he says, that when he speaks of the infinite modes as eternal, what he really means is that they are sempiternal (I, pp. 376–377). His evidence is that in *E* IP21, where Spinoza mentions the infinite modes for the first time in the *Ethics*, he says: "Whatever follows from the absolute nature of any attribute of God must *always* exist and be infinite, or [*sive*] through that same attribute is eternal and infinite." The word "always" [*semper*] suggests temporality, omnitemporality, to be sure, but temporality nonetheless.

Such solutions may be left to those whom they satisfy. The point remains that whatever follows logically from something which is logically necessary must itself be logically necessary. If Spinoza regards the existence and causality of God as being strictly logically necessary, then he has to say that the infinite modes are eternal, whether he wants to or not.

Secondly, and this affects the plausibility of the system, not its consistency, many contemporary philosophers would hold that the laws of nature cannot be logically necessary on the grounds that they are informative. They tell us how things are, whereas logically necessary propositions give us no information about the nature of things. We know nothing about the weather when we know that it either is or is not raining. We know nothing about bodies when we know that they are either in motion or at rest. When Spinoza does give us an example of a law that seems to have some content, as when he cites the law that "all bodies, when they strike other smaller bodies, lose as much of their motion as they communicate to the others," it is difficult to see how the law could be regarded as logically necessary. We would like to see the proof.

Moreover, it will be contended, the reason why logical truths, and analytic truths generally, are uninformative is that they are true simply in virtue of the meanings of their terms. Their truth is guaranteed by the conventional rules of the language in which they are expressed. Since analytic truths depend for their truth only on those rules, and not on the existence of any particular state of affairs in the world, they can say nothing about the world. They do not describe the nature of things, they reflect the prescriptive rules of language.

This, doubtless, is a very common view today. And though it has its critics, I shall not join them now. What interests me here is that the objection which arises from this view of analytic truth forces us to consider how Spinoza conceived of definitions and what he thought their status was. Once we do this, I think we will see that Spinoza's notion of definition is very far removed from that which most contemporary philosophers have. As a result, what is implied when he says that something follows from the definition of a thing is very different from what would be implied on a more conventional account.

The question of the nature of definition is raised in Spinoza's correspondence by Simon de Vries, who invites Spinoza to choose between two conceptions (*Ep.* 8, IV:39–40): the first, that of Giovanni Borelli, a more or less orthodox Aristotelian, according to whom definitions must be true, primary, clearly known to us, and essential, since they are needed as premises in demonstrations; the second, that of Christopher Clavius, according to whom definitions are formulas of human construction (*artis*

*vocabula*), which need not be justified so long as we do not affirm
the thing defined of anything which we have not first shown to possess
the defining characteristics. On this second view, a definition need not
be true, primary, or best known to us.

Spinoza replies that there are two kinds of definition (*Ep.* 9,
IV:42–44): (1) those which explain a thing insofar as it exists outside
the intellect; these must give a true description of their object and do
not differ from propositions or axioms, except in that definitions are
concerned with the essences of things or of affections of things, whereas
propositions or axioms are more general and include eternal truths;[14]
(2) those which explain a thing insofar as we conceive it or can conceive
it; they are not appropriately characterized as true or false, nor are
they susceptible of proof. Spinoza does not say that definitions that explain a thing as it exists outside the intellect must be primary or best
known to us. Here he insists only that they be true.

What Spinoza is giving us is a version of the traditional distinction
between real and nominal definitions. And I think it may be helpful
here if we pause for a moment to compare his classification of the different kinds of definition with that in the *Port-Royal Logic* (pp. 86–99;
164–167). Arnauld and Nicole recognize three fundamentally different
kinds of definition. Two are species of nominal definition (*définition
du nom*); one is real definition (*définition de la chose*):

(1) The first sort of nominal definition, which corresponds roughly
to what would today be called *stipulative definition,* occurs when a
writer assigns a meaning to a word as the meaning it will have in his
discourse. Words in themselves are indifferent and may be made to
signify anything. So writers have freedom of stipulation. This sort of
definition is arbitrary, cannot be contested, and may be taken without
any further justification as a first principle, provided that the writer
makes his usage clear and sticks to it.

(2) The second sort of nominal definition, which corresponds roughly
to what would today be called a *lexical definition,* occurs when a writer
explains what a word means according to the ordinary usage of some
language. Such definitions are not arbitrary. However, they are required
to represent not the truth of things, but the truth of usage. Their job

is to connect the word with the idea people commonly connect it with, and their truth or falsity hangs on whether or not they do this.

(3) The third kind of definition is *real definition*. Here the notion seems to be that one treats the word defined as having its ordinary meaning, as being linked with the idea it is commonly linked with, and then asserts that certain other ideas are contained in (implied by) that idea. This kind of definition is not arbitrary, for it does not depend on man's will that ideas imply what they do. Hence, definitions which are proposed as real definitions can be contested and cannot be taken as first principles without some justification. Unless they are as clear as axioms, they require proof. Arnauld and Nicole say much that is interesting about these different types of definition. They point out, for instance, that though we are free to stipulate any meaning we like for a word it is not always advisable to exercise this freedom. In general they take the position that an established usage should not be changed unless there is something unclear about it, and that when we do introduce a new usage, it should not be too far removed either from the existing usage or from the etymology of the word. They also have some very suggestive things to say about the difficulty of giving adequate lexical definitions.

But the point which is of the greatest importance for our purposes is that they insist quite strongly on the need for distinguishing clearly between stipulative definitions and real ones. The former never need justification, the latter often do. It then becomes crucial to see what the criteria are for a good real definition.

And it is at this stage that Arnauld and Nicole are neither clear nor helpful. They are Aristotelian and Cartesian. The requirements they lay down for a good real definition are as follows:

(1) A good definition should be both universal and proper—by which they mean that it should give the essential attributes of the thing, that is, state necessary and sufficient conditions for being that thing, or a thing of that kind.

They seem to think of this as being done in traditional genus and difference fashion, though they give as examples of successful real definitions a very mixed lot of propositions: man is a rational animal, mind is a thinking substance, body is an extended substance, God is the perfect being. They maintain that the genus in the definition should be the proximate genus of the thing defined, not a remote genus.

(2) A good definition should be clear—by which they mean that it should give us a clearer and more distinct idea of the thing defined and help us to understand the nature of the thing in such a way that we can give an acccount of its principal properties. The combination of requirements is interesting. If we had only the first, it might be possible to represent real definition as being only a confused version of lexical definition. So we might argue: to say that animality and rationality are the essential attributes of man is just a misleading way to say that the word "man" correctly applies to something if and only if the terms "animal" and "rational" correctly apply to it. The supposed real definition is covertly a statement about correct usage.

But however this argument might go, it is clear from the second requirement that we have here a demand for something more than a statement about usage. For we are supposed to pick out a set of characteristics which not only is common and peculiar to the kind of thing in question, but also enables us to explain any other characteristics common and peculiar to that kind of thing ("property" is being used here in the special Aristotelian sense). This is hardly a job for that harmless drudge, the lexicographer.

Now I do not wish to suggest that Spinoza would accept all, or even very much, of this account of definition. He may be said to recognize two of Arnauld and Nicole's three types of definition: the stipulative, to which correspond his definitions that explain a thing as we conceive it or can conceive it; and the real, to which correspond his definitions that explain a thing as it exists outside the intellect. He does not mention lexical definitions. But he does agree that stipulative definitions are arbitrary and need no justification, while real definitions are not arbitrary and do not differ fundamentally from propositions or axioms.

When it comes to the requirements that a good real definition must satisfy, Spinoza would agree that a definition should state the essence of a thing. But he rejects, as we have seen earlier, the traditional technique of defining by genus and difference. The requirements he does make differ for different kinds of definition. Simplifying somewhat, we can say that the definition of a created thing (that is, a thing whose essence does not involve existence, a mode) must

(1) give the proximate cause of the thing, and

(2) suffice for the deduction of all the properties of the thing. (*TdIE*, 96–97, II: 35–36)

The definition of an uncreated thing (that is, a thing whose essence does involve existence, an attribute) must

(1) exclude every cause by making it clear that the thing requires nothing for its explanation beyond its own being and,

(2) leave no room for the question whether the thing exists and,

(3) suffice for the deduction of all the thing's properties.

Spinoza illustrates this conception of definition with the following example. A circle is badly defined as any figure in which lines drawn from the center to the circumference are equal. For this does not give the essence of a circle but only one of its properties. A circle is well defined as that figure which is described by any line of which one end is fixed and the other moving. For this definition gives the proximate cause and suffices for the deduction of such properties of circles as the one given in the bad definition.

It is interesting that Spinoza's example should come from mathematics. Circles, and mathematical entities generally, are classed by Spinoza as entities of reason. They are not real things. They are the same, he says, however they are defined, and it does not much matter how they are defined. With real things it is otherwise. Why not, then, give as an example a definition of a real thing? Spinoza's ostensible reason is that he does not wish to lay bare the errors of others. This is very much in character and is probably correct. But it is natural to suspect that examples would be difficult to find outside of mathematics. The sort of definition Spinoza requires is going to be available, at best, only in the advanced sciences. If we accept the view of Professor H. H. Dubs that the "nuclear equation" of a chemical element is the beginning of a real definition,[15] then there will be real definitions outside of mathematics. But there will not be very many. And they will not be discovered by examining linguistic usage.

It may be objected that if this is what Spinoza has in mind when he speaks of definition—the search for a cause which will explain a thing's properties—then definition is a legitimate and valuable activity, but one which is ill-named. For to call this activity "definition" leads us to think that we need not make "the empirical tests appropriate to all theories about causes."[16]

The point is well taken. I am not certain, however, that Spinoza himself was misled in this way. He speaks, for instance, in the *Theological-Political Treatise,* of the interpretation of nature as consisting in the systematic study (*concinnanda*) of the history of nature, "from which we infer the definitions of natural things . . . nature does not give us definitions of natural things . . . they must be inferred from the diverse actions of nature" (*TTP* 7, III:98–99). It is difficult to know quite how to relate such statements to Spinoza's over-all theory of knowledge, but they certainly must be taken into account when we are considering his theory of definition.

I suggested at the beginning of this discussion that once we saw how Spinoza conceived of definitions we would see why he thought they described the nature of things. The real definitions which his science would employ would not be true simply in virtue of linguistic usage. And so the charge that his nomological propositions are vacuous must fail.

But only at a price. Once we see that definitions, real ones, at any rate, are not merely the expression of human conventions, we can see how they may be informative. They depend for their truth not only on our rules for the use of language, but also on the existence of the states of affairs they purport to describe. Nevertheless, now there no longer seems any reason to regard them as necessary. To question them is not just to show ignorance of the way words are used, it is to raise substantive doubts about the nature of things. To call them definitions at all is probably a mistake, tending only to confusion.

Shall we conclude, then, that the basic nomological facts are contingent, not necessary, sempiternal only, and not eternal? I am not sure. It seems to me that Spinoza could argue—or that we could argue on his behalf—that the very independence which characterizes these facts is itself a sufficient reason for calling them necessary. When we say that something is contingent, etymology suggests, and ordinary use confirms, that we ordinarily understand this to be a relative notion. We mean that there is another thing on which our something is contingent or dependent. To speak of something which is contingent, but which is not contingent on anything, is, in this everyday use of the word, unintelligible. If so, then the basic nomological facts can hardly be called contingent.

This point may be approached in a slightly different way by considering what, in one common case, we mean when we say that something could have been otherwise. Suppose there has been an accident. A car has smashed into a tree and the people inside have been injured. We may say, consolingly, "Ah well, it could have been worse—at least they were wearing their seat-belts." By this I take it that we mean "If they had not been wearing their seat-belts, it would have been worse." Under the circumstances, that is, given the existing background conditions, such as the velocity of the car, the fact that the dashboard was not padded, and so on, and given that the laws of nature are what they are, the fact that they were wearing seat-belts was a sufficient condition of their not being injured more seriously. And under those circumstances, the fact that they were not wearing seat-belts—had it been a fact—would have been a sufficient condition of their being injured more seriously. To say that something could have been otherwise, in this sense, is to say that under certain roughly specifiable conditions it would have been otherwise.

In this very natural sense, the basic nomological facts could not have been otherwise. For there is nothing by which we may explain their being the way they are, nothing which, had it been otherwise, would have led to different results.

It might be objected that, on the account I have given of Spinoza, this is not true. There is something which, had it been otherwise, would have led to different results. The attributes (the basic nomological facts) are a sufficient condition of their infinite modes (the derivative nomological facts), even if they are not a sufficient condition of their finite modes (the singular facts). But wherever $p$ is a sufficient condition of $q$, $q$ is a necessary condition of $p$. So we shall have to say that the derivative nomological facts are a necessary condition of the basic nomological facts. That is, if the derivative nomological facts had been different, the basic nomological facts would have been different.

I reject the premise that wherever $p$ is a sufficient condition of $q$, $q$ is a necessary condition of $p$. This is, I realize, a very common view. But it is an absurd one. Consider the case of the accident. We said that, under the circumstances, the fact that they were wearing a seat-belt was a sufficient condition of the fact that they were not injured more seriously. Shall we say that the fact that they were not injured more seriously was, therefore, a necessary condition of the fact that they wore their seat-belts? But it was not a condition of their wearing their seat-belts at all. This is simply a case where the common philosophical usage is perverse. One fact cannot be a condition of another, in the sense required here, unless it is in some way (logically or temporally) prior to the other.

There is a more fundamental objection to my argument. I have explained the notion of necessity, in the sense in which I wish to apply it to the basic nomological facts, in terms of "could not have been otherwise." And I have suggested that something could not have been otherwise, in this sense, if there are no circumstances under which it would have been otherwise. It will no doubt be objected that the concepts which I have used to explain necessity are at least as obscure as the concept of necessity itself. In particular, I have used counterfactual conditionals, and these are widely thought to be very troublesome. I have not, to use the Port-Royal terminology, given a definition of necessity that provides us with a clearer and more distinct idea of the thing defined.

This general line of argument will be familiar to any reader of W. V. O. Quine's "Two Dogmas of Empiricism," and I am afraid there is no way out of the kind of dilemma Quine presents. When we undertake to explain a modal concept, like necessity, we must use either terms which are unobjectionable, but not logically strong enough to do the job, or terms which are logically strong enough, but equally difficult. (Or nearly so. Counterfactual conditionals are not quite as obscure as "could have been otherwise." In English, "could have been" is very ambiguous.) I am not sure what the moral of this story is. Perhaps we should give up using modal terms. Or perhaps we should revise our expectations as to what a philosopher's explanation can achieve.

At any rate, if the independence of the basic nomological facts, and not their supposed analytic truth, is taken as the ground for calling them necessary, then the objection made earlier about the necessity of the infinite modes can be dealt with. The problem was that what follows from something which is logically necessary must itself be logically necessary. But what follows from, or depends on, something which is necessary in the sense of being absolutely independent is not itself necessary in that sense. Quite the contrary.

There will, on this view, be three species of necessity. The first is that possessed by the most general nomological facts, those constituting the nature of the divine attributes. These, since they do not and cannot owe their existence to anything else, possess a necessity which is absolute, unconditional, and atemporal. The necessity of the less general nomological facts, by contrast, is relative and conditional but still atemporal. They do owe their existence to something else, but that to which they owe their existence, the most general facts, is something which is itself absolutely necessary. The necessity of the singular facts is both relative or conditional and temporal. For they always owe their existence both to nomological facts, whose existence is not subject to temporal variation, and to other singular facts, which come into being and pass away as the conditions of their existence are and are not realized. As Spinoza puts it,

> Some things, then, are transient in themselves; others, indeed, are not transient because of their cause. But there is a third which, through its own force and power alone, is eternal and imperishable. The first are all the particular things which have not existed from all time, or which have had a beginning; the second are all the

> [general] modes which we have said are the cause of the par-
> ticular modes; and the third is God, or what we take to be one
> and the same, the Truth. (*KV*, II, v, I:62–63)

In the light of what has been said earlier, this requires little comment.

It will, perhaps, be objected that the existence of the basic nomological
facts is still hardly self-explanatory. But this complaint stems from a
failure to appreciate sufficiently the difference between the two series
of causes: the infinite series of finite causes and the finite series of infinite
causes. As even St. Thomas admitted, there is no reason, apart from
the word of sacred Scripture, to suppose that former series should have
a first member. But it is most implausible to suppose that the explanation
of laws could proceed ad infinitum, passing always to more general
principles under which the lower level ones may be subsumed. And if
we must stop somewhere, then when we reach that point, the demand
for further explanation is unreasonable.

To say this is to accept the view that ultimate explanations of a
sort are in principle possible. It is not to say that any explanation we
now have is ultimate, or that an ultimate explanation must be intuitively
evident. We may well agree with Popper that

> it is not truisms which science unveils. Rather, it is part of the
> greatness and beauty of science that we can learn, through our
> own critical investigations, that the world is utterly different from
> what we ever imagined—until our imagination was fired by the
> refutation of our earlier theories,[17]

without accepting his conclusion that the process of conjecture and refu-
tation has no natural end. Thus we might, with the pragmatists, think
of science as a progressive activity, whose explanatory theories converge,
as toward an ideal limit, upon that system of propositions which constitutes the truth about the world in which we live.

I conclude, then, that there is, within the framework of this interpretation, a way of making sense of the eternity, or necessary existence, of
God.

Just what Spinoza meant by these ideas, and how he conceived the mental correlates of bodies and of their motions and changes, is a question that has provoked difference of opinion. Since there are ideas of inanimate as well as animate objects and processes, ideas can scarcely be regarded as individual psychical entities . . . Nor, since for Spinoza, the infinite intellect of God is impersonal, can they be the thoughts of a self-conscious mind reflecting upon the order and connection of physical events. One is tempted rather to think that the *idea* meant for him what we should call the truth about each particular physical event.

—Fuller, *History of Philosophy*

# 4  The Divine Attributes

The interpretation presented so far was designed originally to answer certain questions about substance and its modes: what is substance? what are its modes? how are they related? And I think I can give a tolerably clear and plausible answer to these questions. But if there is anything in this approach to Spinoza, it ought to be capable of being applied to other puzzling areas in his system, and in particular to the problem of the relation between the attributes. In what follows I shall try to show how I believe this can be done.

There are, of course, really two problems about the relation between the attributes of Spinoza's substance. There is the problem of understanding how Spinoza conceived of the relation between thought and extension, and there is the problem of understanding how he conceived the two known attributes of thought and extension to be related to the infinitely many unknown attributes.

## Thought and Extension

Since, as we might expect, Spinoza gives us more information about the two known attributes than about the infinitely many unknown attributes, it will be best to begin by considering their relation. First I shall sketch what looks like a promising way of extending the line of thought so far developed. Then I shall try to show why it won't do. And finally I shall try to work out an alternative which takes better account of the peculiarities of Spinoza's philosophy.

Consider the following proposal. Spinoza, I have suggested, built on the possibility of a unified science of extended objects. There are certain fundamental laws of nature governing the behavior of all extended objects. The various changes in the objects can all ultimately be understood in terms of these laws. Analogously, we might suppose that he recognized as well the existence of nonextended objects, thoughts, volitions, sensations, and the like, and that he envisaged the possibility of a unified science of nonextended objects, a universal psychology, strictly parallel to the universal physics we have been imagining, with fundamental laws of psychic events, derived laws, and nomological explanations of individual psychical phenomena.

We might be struck by the fact that when, in the *Theological-Political Treatise,* Spinoza wants to give examples of laws which depend on natural necessity, he gives one example from physics, a law of impact, and one example from psychology, a law of association. And we might argue that part III of the *Ethics,* which discusses the origin and nature of the human emotions is an attempt to work out the rudiments of this universal psychology.

Confronted with Spinoza's notion that the mode of extension and the idea of that mode are one and the same thing, expressed in two different ways (*E* IIP7cs), we might appeal to the currently popular view that mental events are contingently identical with brain events, that a description of what goes on in us in psychological terms has a different sense than, but the same reference as, the corresponding description in physiological terms. And clearly, there are many passages in Spinoza—particularly those in which he connects the vitality of the mind with the vitality of the body—which would tend to support this sort of approach.

But although the approach described might take us a certain distance, I don't believe that we can get very far with it. It attributes to Spinoza a view which is, perhaps, attractive and plausible, probably more plausible than the one I shall argue for, but it is in many respects a misleading model for interpreting him. To mention only one of its most prominent defects, nothing in this line of interpretation would suggest that for Spinoza there should be a mode of thought for each mode of extension. In fact, this line would suggest rather the opposite.

The view that sensations, thoughts, and so forth are brain processes implies that where you do not find the appropriate physiological structures, you cannot expect to find any mental processes either. Even though my watch is a fairly complicated piece of machinery, you would not expect it to have any sensations. But plainly, Spinoza does think that *every* mode of extension has its corresponding mode of thought, or rather, *is* its corresponding mode of thought:

> The order and connection of ideas is the same as the order and
> connection of things (*E* IIp7) . . . Let us here recall what has
> been proved above, viz., that whatever can be perceived by the in-
> finite intellect as constituting the essence of substance pertains to
> one substance only. Therefore, thinking substance and extended sub-
> stance are one and the same substance, which is now grasped under
> the one attribute and now under the other. So also a mode of
> extension and the idea of that mode are one and the same thing,
> but expressed in two ways . . . For example, a circle existing in
> nature and the idea which is in God of an existing circle are one
> and the same thing, but explained through different attributes.
> (*E* IIp7s)

If my watch, or as I should prefer to say, the fact that my watch has
such and such a character, is a mode of extension, then there is a mode
of thought which is a different expression of the same thing.

This is, to say the least, puzzling. It is almost enough to make one
despair of making sense of Spinoza. But before we despair, let us try
another tack. We have to face the fact that Spinoza intends his terms
"idea" and "mode of thought" to be understood in a way for which
Descartes and Locke have not prepared us.

The first thing to do is to recall what we noted earlier about Spinoza's
ideas involving an element of affirmation. This is something that Spinoza
goes to great pains to emphasize. In defining the term "idea" as a "concept of the mind, which the mind forms because it is a thinking thing"
(*E* IId3), he explains that he uses the term "concept" rather than "perception" because the latter term suggests wrongly that the mind is passive
in relation to its object, not active. Later he enlarges on this when he
warns his readers to distinguish carefully between an idea and an image.
Those, he says,

> who think that ideas consist in images which are formed in us
> through contact with [*NS*: external] bodies, persuade themselves
> that those ideas of things [*NS*: which can make no trace on our

> brains, or] of which we can form no similar images, are not ideas,
> but only inventions, which we feign from a free choice of the will;
> so they think of ideas as of mute pictures on a tablet, and preoccu-
> pied with this prejudice, they do not see that an idea, insofar as
> it is an idea, involves affirmation or negation. (*E* Ip49cs, II:132)

So ideas, for Spinoza, involve an activity of the mind, an activity of
affirmation or negation. Hence, it would be appropriate in most contexts
in Spinoza to substitute the term "proposition" or "assertion" for the
term "idea." By contrast, this would not be appropriate in most contexts
in Descartes or Locke.[1] Spinoza's ideas are the sort of thing that can
follow from and entail one another, that can be true or false in the
traditional sense of agreeing with their object (*E* Ia6).

It is customary, of course, to attribute to Spinoza a coherence theory
of truth. But the reader who feels that I am placing more weight on
*E* Ia6 than that axiom can comfortably bear may find it worthwhile
to reflect on the passage in the *Metaphysical Thoughts* in which Spinoza
discusses the meaning of the terms "true" and "false." The passage
not only supports a correspondence theory of truth, but also is curiously
contemporary in its methodology. Spinoza begins by remarking that

> Since the multitude first invent words, which are afterward taken
> over (*usurpantur*) by the philosophers, it seems appropriate for
> one who seeks the original signification of any word to ask what
> it first denoted among the multitude—particularly where there is
> a lack of any other explanations which, from the nature of the lan-
> guage, could be brought forward for investigating the signification.
> (*CM* I, vi, I:246)

We might note in passing that Spinoza works on the same methodologi-
cal principle in the preface to part IV of the *Ethics,* where he undertakes
to give an account of the meaning of the terms "perfect" and "imperfect" and "good" and "evil." Spinoza continues:

The original signification of "true" and "false" seems to have
arisen from narratives: they called a narrative true which was of
a deed which had really happened (*quae erat facti quod revera
contigerat*), and false when it was of a deed which had not happened. And this signification the philosophers afterward took over
to denote the agreement between an idea and its object (*ideatum*),
and the opposite.

As a piece of amateur lexicography, this is remarkably suggestive. People
who wonder about the meaning of some word are often counseled to
consider how they would teach a child to use it. And it seems to me
that it is generally in the context of stories that children are first introduced to the concept of truth. In any case, Spinoza concludes that "an
idea is true if it shows us the thing as it is in itself and false if it shows
us the thing as other than it really is. For ideas are nothing but mental
narratives or histories of nature." I have rendered the term *factum* in
this passage as "deed." "Fact," which H. H. Britan uses, strikes me
as anachronistic. For as far as I have been able to discover, the Latin
term never had the technical sense that its English cognate has.[2] Perhaps
this is why Spinoza had to coin the term *"ideatum"* for that with which
a true idea agrees.

Earlier I used the assertional character of Spinoza's ideas to argue
that their correlates in the attribute of extension, the *ideata* with which
true ideas are said to agree (*E* IA6), ought to be construed as facts
rather than as things. Now I want to suggest that we can do reasonable
justice to Spinoza's concept of the relation between thought and extension if we think of the relation between thought and extension as an
identity of true proposition and fact. It is misleading to say, even though
Spinoza himself says it, that a true idea agrees with the object (read
"a true proposition agrees with the fact"), because the mode of extension
and the idea of that mode are one and the same thing expressed in
two different ways. The fact and the true proposition are the same
thing, expressed or viewed in two different ways. To talk about a mode

as a proposition or idea, bearing logical relations to other propositions, is to conceive the mode under the attribute of thought. To talk about it as a fact, having causal relations with other facts, is to conceive it under the attribute of extension. But the propositions which make up the set that gives a complete and accurate description of the world are identical with the facts they describe, and the causal relations between the facts have their counterpart in the logical relations between propositions.

This is how I propose to read Spinoza's doctrine that "the order and connection of ideas is the same as the order and connection of things" (*E* IIP7). Spinoza thinks that this proposition is obvious from *E* IA4, according to which "knowledge of an effect depends on and involves knowledge of its cause." For, he says, "the idea of anything which is caused depends on the knowledge of the cause whose effect it is" (*E* IIP7D). This is to say that wherever you have two facts standing in a causal relation you also have two propositions standing in a logical relation, the proposition describing the cause entailing the one describing the effect. The set of true propositions is the world conceived under the attribute of thought; the set of facts, the world conceived under the attribute of extension. But the two worlds are not two, they are one.

So far, I suspect, my explanation of what Spinoza means must seem quite as mysterious as the doctrine it is designed to explain. But I think I can enlarge on what I have said in a way that will be helpful. As I am here using the notions of fact and proposition, propositions are related to facts in roughly the way that, in Aristotle, form is related to matter. The analogy runs as follows: for Aristotle, a concrete object is a unity which is separable for purposes of thought into two elements, the form, or universal element, which is capable of characterizing many objects, and the matter, or particular element, which makes the object *this* particular object. Let us say that a concrete situation is also analyzable into two elements, an abstract pattern which can characterize many situations and a particularizing element which makes it *this* particular situation. Thus, if it is a fact that Mary is making pies, then this fact is a particular instance of a type of situation that could have many instances. There are, or could be, many situations of which the sentence "Mary is making pies" might be truly affirmed. Call the abstract pattern common to all these the proposition. Call the particularizing element the fact.[3]

There is a difficulty about this analogy. The relation of form to matter in Aristotle is a many-one relation. A plurality of forms may characterize one and the same object. The same might be said of the relation between propositions and facts. For normally we should wish to say that one and the same fact might be truly described by a number of distinct propositions. For example, at one stage during the process of Mary's making her pies, it was true that

(1) Mary is rotating the dial on the stove and,
(2) She is turning on the electricity in the oven and,
(3) She is starting to heat the oven.

These sentences are not logically equivalent, and so express different propositions. But many people would have a strong temptation to say that they are all true in virtue of one and the same fact.[4] What is difficult about this is that Spinoza's system requires the relation between modes of thought and modes of extension to be a one-one relation.

In this case I am not sure that our instinct to speak of three different descriptions of the same fact is correct. Mary might have rotated the dial without turning on the electricity (if there had been a faulty connection); and she might have turned on the electricity without rotating the dial (if the circuit had been closed, say, by her activating a photoelectric cell as she approached the stove). So it is not clear to me that the truth-conditions of (1) are the same as the truth-conditions of (2). (1) is rendered true by something she did to the dial. (2) is rendered true by the fact that when she did this to the dial, something else happened—namely, the circuit was closed.

The question "What are the identity conditions for facts?" is a very obscure one. I think a great many people who have held correspondence theories of truth have supposed—rightly or wrongly—that there are just as many facts as there are distinct true propositions. Whether or not this is so, it is the sort of view we need for interpreting Spinoza. If it does violence to our ordinary notion of what a fact is, so be it.

In interpreting Spinoza's doctrine that the mode of extension and its idea are one as equivalent to the claim that facts and true propositions are one, in the sense described, I am saying, in effect, that on this point Wolfson is right. Wolfson recommends that we understand Spinoza's theory of the mind-body relationship as differing only in terminology from the Aristotelian view that the soul is the form of the body (II, 36–64). And I think that this is substantially correct. It is not quite right, because we have to extend the notion of form and matter in the way done above in order to allow for Spinoza's emphasis on the assertional element in ideas. And we have to make further adjustments to allow for the relation's being one-to-one. But only in a way like this can we account for Spinoza's notion that there is a mode of thought for every mode of extension. Spinoza's statement that "all things are animate, though in different degrees," that "there must be in God an idea of everything" (*E* IIP13CS), does not imply that my watch has thoughts and sensations, any more than Aristotle's doctrine that plants have souls implies that flowers feel pain.

Suppose that the fact that my watch is made of gold is a mode of the attribute of extension. Then the true proposition that my watch is made of gold is a mode of the attribute of thought. The true proposition is the idea in thought of the mode of extension, it is its form, or, if you like, its mind. I think Spinoza would be willing enough to say this. When he says that the human mind is the idea of the human body (*E* IIP13), he is not crediting the human body with anything that any other mode of extension does not have.

But to say that for every mode of extension there is a corresponding mode of thought is not to attribute consciousness to all things. Spinoza implies quite plainly that such things as stones do not possess consciousness (see *Ep.* 58, IV: 266). My watch does not know that it is made of gold. Apparently it is not a sufficient condition of consciousness that there exist in thought an idea of a mode of extension; it is necessary also that there exist in thought an idea of that idea. Knowledge or consciousness arises only where the mind contains not merely ideas of the affections of the body, but also ideas of those ideas.

This point is not stated very clearly in Spinoza, but it does come out, I think, on a close reading of *E* IIp11–30. For example, in *E* IIp12, Spinoza says:

> Whatever happens in the object of the idea constituting the human mind must be perceived by the human mind, that is, an idea of the thing will necessarily exist in the mind. In other words, if the object of the idea constituting the human mind is a body, nothing can happen in the body which is not perceived by the mind [*NS*: or of which there is not a thought in the soul].

We are told by the following proposition that the object of the idea constituting a human mind *is* a body—and, moreover, it appears from *E* IIp16c2 that the object of the idea constituting a human mind is the body which is united with that mind: "The ideas we have of external bodies indicate the constitution of our own body more than the nature of external bodies." In terms of the current interpretation, this series of doctrines could be stated in the following way: my body is a set of facts, my mind a set of propositions describing those facts; my mind must contain a proposition corresponding to every fact that constitutes my body, for the propositions simply are the facts, considered in a different way.

One might infer from this the surprising doctrine that the mind is aware or conscious of everything that goes on in the body. That seems, on the face of it, to be what *E* IIp12 is saying. If so, doctors' jobs would be a good deal easier than they are. Your doctor would not have to take a blood test to see if your white corpuscle count was down; he could simply ask you. This is absurd, and we should require very good evidence before we attribute such a doctrine to Spinoza.

In the first place, let me say that I think some significance may be attached to the fact that in the wording of *E* IIp12 Spinoza uses the verb "perceive" rather than "know." This suggests the possibility that, although nothing can happen in the body which the mind does not perceive, there may be things happening in the body of which the mind is not aware or conscious.

This suggestion is confirmed, I think, in *E* IIP19, when Spinoza says that "the human mind does not know the human body itself, nor does it know that the body exists, except through ideas of affections by which the body is affected." I take this as meaning that it is not simply in having an idea of an affection of the body that the mind knows the body—rather it is by means of that idea that the mind knows the body. "When we say that the human mind perceives this or that, we say nothing but that God has this or that idea, not insofar as he is infinite, but insofar as he is explained through the nature of the human mind, or insofar as he constitutes the essence of the human mind" (*E* IIP11C). To say that God has this or that idea is simply to say there is in God a mode of extension which may also be regarded, under the attribute of thought, as a mode of thought, that is, a fact which may also be regarded as a proposition. It is only when something else is added to the mind's "perception" of the body that consciousness arises.

The nature of this something else is explained in *E* IIP20–23, where Spinoza introduces the concept of an idea of an idea. *E* IIP22, for example, tells us that "the human mind perceives not only the affections of the body, but also the ideas of these affections," that is, that it contains not only ideas of bodily modifications, but also ideas of these ideas. And *E* IIP23 says that "the mind does not know itself except insofar as it perceives the ideas of the affections of the body," that is, except insofar as it has ideas of ideas. We can equate having an idea of an idea with being conscious. *E* IIP19 and *E* IIP23 together, then, say that the mind does not know the body except insofar as it perceives itself, or has ideas of ideas, or is conscious. It is worth noting in this connection that, while every individual thing has a "mind" containing ideas of the affections of its body (*E* IIP13S), the existence of ideas of ideas is proven only for human minds (*E* IIP20). I infer from this that, although Spinoza is willing to assert that everything is animate (in a very odd sense of the term), he is not prepared to say that anything except a human being is conscious.

It may be helpful to think of an idea of an idea as a proposition about another proposition. Since I am identifying the possession of an idea of an idea with consciousness, it seems natural to say that an idea of an idea is a special kind of proposition about a proposition, namely, one expressing what is sometimes called a propositional attitude (for example, "*A* knows that *p*").

As soon as we formulate it this way, however, we seem to run into difficulty. The idea that is the object of my idea of an idea will have as its ideatum a modification of my body and it will agree with that modification. This amounts, on my interpretation, to saying that what I know when I know that something is the case is a proposition which describes some fact about my body. And this would certainly be a very strange doctrine. For surely we would want to say that relatively few of the propositions I know are propositions describing facts about my body. How is it then that I can know propositions which describe facts about bodies other than my own?

Again, this probem does not arise simply because of my peculiar way of formulating Spinoza's doctrines. It is there in Spinoza,[5] as the following passage shows:

> We understand clearly what is the difference between the idea of Peter which constitutes the esssence of the mind of Peter and the idea of Peter which is in another man, say Paul. For the former explains directly the essence of the body of Peter himself, and does not involve existence except as long as Peter exists; the latter, on the other hand, indicates the constitution of the body of Paul more than the nature of Peter. (*E* IIp17cs, II:105–106)

We can frame essentially the same question in Spinoza's own language: How is it that the idea of Peter which is in Paul is appropriately described as an idea of Peter when what it agrees with is a modification of Paul's body?

Readers who come to Spinoza from a study of the British empiricists will naturally feel tempted to answer this query by saying that Paul's

idea of Peter, though it may in some sense correspond to a modification
of Paul's body, is properly an idea of Peter because it is a representation
of Peter, a mental image of him. Spinoza quite explicitly rules this out
in a number of places. Ideas are not images. Indeed, Spinoza is willing
to apply the term "image" only to certain modifications of the body,
and even these he does not think of as pictures of something external:

> To keep the customary vocabulary, we shall call the affections
> of the human body whose ideas represent external bodies as present
> to us images of things, although they do not reproduce the forms
> of things. (*E* IIp17s)
>
> By ideas I understand, not images of the sort formed at the
> base of the eye, and if you please, in the middle of the brain,
> but concepts of thought [*NS*: or the objective essence of a thing,
> insofar as it exists only in thought]. (*E* IIp48s, cf. *E* IIp49s)

Clearly we cannot think of Paul's idea of Peter as a mental image of
Peter, or even as the mental correlate of a bodily image of Peter. But
how, then, is it an idea of Peter?

Our question has an answer, if not a satisfactory one. *E* IIp16–17
gives us the justification for saying that an idea that "indicates" the
constitution of Paul's body is an idea of Peter: the idea in Paul's mind
has as an object a modification of Paul's body that "involves" the nature
of Peter. But what is it for a modification of Paul's body to involve
Peter's nature? We get a clue in *E* IIp17d:

> As long as the human body is affected [in a way which involves
> the nature of some external body], so long will the human mind
> contemplate this affection of the body, that is, it will have an idea
> of an actually existing mode which involves the nature of the ex-
> ternal body, an idea which does not exclude the existence or
> presence of the nature of the external body, but asserts it.

From this we can say that when a modification of the human body
is caused by an external body (or one of the modifications of that body),

the modification of the human body involves the nature of the external
body, and the idea of this modification asserts the existence of the nature
of the external body (in addition to agreeing with its own immediate
object). This is a bit vague, to be sure, but there is further help later on:

> The ideas of the affections of the human body involve the nature
> of external bodies as well as the nature of its own body (*E* IIp16),
> and they must involve not only the nature of the human body,
> but also the nature of its parts, for the affections are ways in which
> the parts of the human body, and consequently, the body as a
> whole, are affected (*E* II post. 3). But (*E* IIp24–25) an adequate
> knowledge of external bodies and of the parts composing the human
> body does not exist in God insofar as he is considered as affected
> by the human mind [alone] but [only] insofar as he is affected
> by other ideas [as well] [*NS*: that is (*E* IIp13), this knowledge
> is not in God insofar as he constitutes the nature of the human
> mind]. Therefore, these ideas of affections, insofar as they are re-
> ferred to the human mind alone, are like *conclusions without
> premises*. That is, as is self-evident, they are confused ideas.
> (*E* IIp28D)

This doctrine may be read in the following way: among the propositions
in *A*, there are some which describe the body of Paul; at least some
of these propositions describing facts about Paul will not be deducible
solely from other propositions describing facts about Paul (taken together
with the laws of nature); these propositions will require for their deduction at least some propositions describing facts about bodies external
to Paul's. Suppose that one such proposition, say *p*, requires as a premise
for its deduction from the laws of nature the proposition *q*, where *q*
describes some fact about Peter's body. In such a case we shall say that
*p* involves *q*, which describes Peter's nature[6] and that therefore *p*
"asserts" (*ponit*) the existence of the nature of Peter's body. That is,
it affirms the existence of something of that nature. In this instance,
*p* would be an idea which primarily indicates the constitution of Paul's
body, but is also an idea of Peter.

If this is a correct account of how Spinoza thought that we have knowledge of the external world, then we can begin to see why he regarded that knowledge as necessarily inadequate. We have ideas of the external world in having ideas of modifications of our bodies which cannot be understood solely through other modifications of our bodies, but only through the modifications of other bodies. And to say this is *ipso facto* to say that these ideas are inadequate:

> The human mind is a part of the infinite intellect of God: and therefore, when we say that the human mind perceives this or that, we say nothing but that God has this or that idea, not insofar as he is infinite, but insofar as he is explained through the nature of the human mind, or insofar as he constitutes the essence of the human mind. And when we say that God has this or that idea, not only insofar as he constitutes the nature of the human mind, but also insofar as he has, with the human mind, the idea of some other thing, then we say that the human mind perceives partially or inadequately. (*E* IIp11c)

To put this in my terms: the human mind is a proper subset, $M$, of the totality of true propositions, $A$; to say that the mind perceives $p$ is to say that $p$ is a member of $M$; whenever $p$ cannot be deduced from other members of $M$ alone, but only from them in conjunction with members of $A$ which are not members of $M$, then $p$ is an inadequate idea. Since it is necessarily the case, whenever $p$ is an idea of an external body, that $p$ cannot be deduced from other members of $M$ alone, sense perception must give inadequate knowledge. But in God, all ideas are adequate. That is, the totality of true propositions, $A$, forms a system. Every proposition in it (except the axioms of scientific theory) follows from other propositions in the system.

Thus when Spinoza wishes to show that our knowledge of the duration of our body can only be very inadequate (*E* IIp30), he argues in the following way:

1. The duration of our body does not depend on its essence (*E* IIA1), nor on the absolute nature of God (*E* Ip21).

1a. The fact that *a* exists, where *a* is a human body, is not absolutely necessary, nor does it follow from the laws of nature alone.

2. Rather it is determined to exist and act by [*NS*: other] causes, of a kind which are also determined by other things to exist and act in a fixed and definite way, and these things by others, and so on, to infinity (*E* Ip28).

2a. Rather the fact that *a* exists, is only relatively necessary, that is, necessary given (the nomological facts in conjunction with) other singular facts, each of which is itself only relatively necessary.

3. Therefore, the duration of our body depends on the common order of nature, and on the constitution of things.

3a. The fact that a given human body exists, therefore, depends (partly) on the existence and nature of other finite things.

4. Moreover, of the reason why things are so constituted, there is an adequate knowledge in God, insofar as he has the idea of all things, and not only insofar as he has the idea of the human body (*E* IIp9c).

4a. A complete explanation of any singular proposition in *A* is possible for one who knows all other (prior) singular propositions in *A*, but not for one who knows only some proper subset of them.

5. Therefore, the knowledge of the duration of our body is quite inadequate in God insofar as he is considered as constituting only the nature of the human mind, that is, the knowledge of the duration of our body is quite inadequate in our mind (*E* IIp11c).

5a. Therefore, the proposition that *a* exists does not follow from the subset of *A* which constitutes the mind of *a*.

In the following proposition (*E* IIP31), Spinoza demonstrates, by the same line of reasoning, the same result for our knowledge of the duration of all external singular things.

Not all knowledge, of course, is inadequate in this way. Whenever we are determined externally to perceive something, our perception of it is inadequate. But sometimes, Spinoza thinks, we are determined internally to have a certain idea, and then our idea will be an adequate one (*E* IIP29S). The reason why this is possible, apparently, is that the common notions, which are "equally in the part and in the whole," cannot be conceived except adequately (*E* IIP38). These ideas must be adequate in the human mind, not just in God. And whatever follows from ideas that are adequate in the human mind must also be adequate in the human mind (*E* IIP40). So, whenever an idea in the human mind follows from the common notions and from other previous ideas in the human mind, that idea will be internally determined, and consequently, adequate.

This account of what is required for an idea to be adequate may help to explain why Spinoza attached the ethical importance he did to the possession of adequate ideas. For to the extent that our ideas are in this way internally determined, we are the adequate cause of our affections (*E* IIID1), and hence, active rather than passive (*E* IIID2). And it is the active life which constitutes virtue itself (*E* IVP22–24).

But the account is not without its difficulties. For one thing, it is not easy to see why Spinoza should have supposed that ideas which are in this sense adequate should also be adequate in the sense of possessing all the properties, or intrinsic denominations, of a true idea (*E* IID4), that is, that they should be clear and distinct. Spinoza seems to be working with two definitions of adequacy, and I know of no argument to show that one may be reduced to the other.

More important, perhaps, it is not easy to see how, on the interpretation I have given of the relation between thought and extension, the system can allow for the existence of false ideas. If a true idea simply *is* the fact it correctly describes, a false idea must be one which describes no fact, a mode of thought which has no corresponding mode of extension. But like form without matter, that is an impossibility.

I am not sure whether this is a difficulty in the interpretation or simply a difficulty in the system. There is at least one sense in which Spinoza does deny the existence of false ideas. In *E* IIp32D, he argues that "Every idea which is in God agrees entirely with its [*NS*: object and] ideatum (*E* IIp7c), and therefore, every idea which is in God is true (*E* IA6)." Since whatever is is in God (*E* Ip15), and therefore every idea is in God, this would appear to entail that every idea, without qualification, is true.

There is some problem in knowing what to make of the phrase "which is in God." I suspect that what Spinoza has in mind is something like this. Every idea, or at least every idea which is an idea of an external object, may be considered in either of two ways—either in relation to what we might call its primary object, the mode which is its correlate in the attribute of extension, or in relation to its secondary object, the mode which caused its extensional correlate. Thus Paul's idea of Peter has as its primary object a modification of Paul's body and as its secondary object a modification of Peter's body. Considered in relation to its primary object, that is, as an "idea in God," it is, necessarily, true. But considered in relation to its secondary object, that is, as an "idea in us," it need not be true. This interpretation of the phrase "idea which is in God" seems to be confirmed by a passage in the *Short Treatise*:

> Between the idea and the object, there must necessarily be a union, since the one cannot exist without the other; for there is nothing of which there is not an idea in the thinking thing, and no idea can exist unless the thing exists . . . But it is necessary to note that we are here speaking of the ideas which arise necessarily in God of the existence of things, together with their essences, not of the ideas which the things now actually present to us and produce in us. The two differ greatly. For in God the ideas do not

arise as they do in us, from one or more of the senses, through
which we are nearly always very imperfectly affected by the things,
but from their existence and essence, that is, from all that they are.
(*KV*, II, xx, I:97).

But even if we grant that Spinoza does want to make a distinction
of this sort between "ideas in God" and "ideas in us," it is still not
clear what account we are to give of false ideas. I suggested above that
Paul's idea of Peter was an idea of Peter in virtue of the fact that
the modification of Paul's body which is its primary object was caused
by the modification of Peter which is its secondary object; Paul's idea
not only characterizes a modification of his body, but also affirms the
existence of something else of a sort sufficient to produce that modification. This does not leave much room for error. If it *is* an idea of Peter,
that is, if the corresponding modification of Paul's body *was* caused
by a modification of Peter's body, then the thing whose existence it affirms
must exist. It is, therefore, a true idea both with respect to its primary
object and with respect to its secondary object. If, on the other hand,
there is nothing external which has produced this particular modification
of Paul's body, then it just is not an idea of anything external to Paul.

This, again, seems to be a conclusion which Spinoza cheerfully accepted. "The imaginations of the mind, considered in themselves, contain no error" (*E* IIp17s). "There is nothing positive in ideas on account
of which they are called false" (*E* IIp33). Falsity, or error, for Spinoza,
consists not in our having an idea which fails to agree with its object,
but solely in our not having as well other ideas of the object which
we might have had. A characteristic example which he gives is that
of the error some are supposed to make in thinking the sun to be about
two hundred feet away from us (*E* IIp35s). The basis for this opinion
lies partly in the fact that our bodies are affected in a certain way
by the sun, that is, in the way in which the body typically is affected
by large, bright, distant objects, and partly in the fact that our bodies
are not affected by the sun in such a way as to exclude the possibility

of certain distances. The error lies in the partiality of our idea of the object, in our not being affected by it in as many ways as are abstractly possible. Thus Spinoza writes, in the *Short Treatise,*

> When someone acquires a form or mode of thinking as a result
> of an action on him by the whole of an object, it is clear that
> he has an altogether different perception of the form and nature
> of this object than someone else, who has not had so many causes
> and so is moved to affirm or deny something about the object
> by a different and lesser action, since he has perceived the object
> by means of fewer or slighter affections. (*KV*, II, xv, I:79; cf.
> *KV*, II, xvi, I:83–84)

It is solely in terms of a difference in degree of awareness of the object that Spinoza undertakes to account for the difference between true and false belief about the object.

What seems to have motivated this view—apart from the internal logic of the Spinozistic system—is the observation that even after we have corrected an erroneous judgment about a perceptual object we do not alter our original perception of it. The sun still looks the same to us even when we know that its distance from us is equal to several hundred times the diameter of the earth. But Spinoza's theory of error still does not strike me as a very satisfactory one. For it seems to obliterate the distinction we should normally wish to make between error and ignorance. Spinoza identifies believing that the sun is only two hundred feet away with not believing that it is much further away. But surely the two states of mind are very different.

There remains to be discussed (at least) one major problem in interpreting Spinoza's account of the relation between mind and body, and that is the notoriously difficult question of what Spinoza intended by his doctrine of the eternity of the mind. This is ground on which the prudent commentator will hestitate to tread, for there is some reason to think that here Spinoza himself was conscious that he was not expressing his views as clearly as might be desired. Nevertheless, I think it may be possible to make some headway on the problem.

One would not have expected Spinoza to hold that "the human mind cannot be absolutely destroyed with the body" (E Vp23). The whole spirit of his theory of the relation of mind to body seems to be to establish the closest possible connection between them, and one would naturally expect that when the body is destroyed the mind would perish with it. But Spinoza clearly thought otherwise. "Something of the mind remains which is eternal" (*E* Vp23). We get a clue to Spinoza's intentions, I think, from the proof which follows this proposition:

> In God there necessarily exists a concept or idea which expresses the essence of the human body (Vp22), and which is, therefore, necessarily something which pertains to the essence of the human mind (IIp13). But we attribute to the human mind no duration which can be defined by time, except insofar as it expresses the actual existence of the body, which is explained through duration, and which can be defined by time, that is (IIp8c), we cannot ascribe duration to the mind except while the body has duration. Nevertheless, since this something is that which is conceived by a certain eternal necessity through the essence itself of God (Vp22), this something, which pertains to the essence of the mind, will necessarily be eternal. (*E* Vp23D)

The key here seems to me to be the third sentence which says, roughly, that the mind only possesses durational existence to the extent that its body does. This does not tell us what we want to know. We want to know how the mind can possess nondurational existence apart from the body. But the citation of IIp8c is more helpful. IIp8 says that

> the ideas of singular things, or of nonexistent modes, must be comprehended in the infinite idea of God, in the same way that the essences of singular things or modes are contained in the attributes of God.

The corollary goes on to add that

> when individual things do not exist unless insofar as they are com-
> prehended in the attributes of God, their objective being or ideas
> do not exist except insofar as the infinite idea of God exists; and
> when individual things are said to exist, not only insofar as they
> are comprehended in God's attributes, but also insofar as they are
> said to have duration, their ideas also involve existence through
> which they are said to have duration.

Now the mind, considered as something which continues to exist after
the destruction of the body, would be an idea of a nonexistent singular
thing or mode. So it would exist as something which is, in Spinoza's
terminology, "comprehended in the infinite idea of God." And the question now is "What is it for an idea to exist as comprehended in the
infinite idea of God?" In *E* IIp8s, Spinoza tries to clarify this notion
by appealing to an analogy which he confesses is not exact. But, he
says, "I cannot give an example which will adequately explain the thing

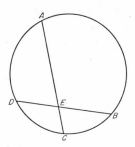

I speak of here, since it is unique." Still, the illustration he does give
seems to be of some help. Imagine a circle, *ABCD*, in which the two
straight lines *AC* and *BD* intersect at a point, *E*. It is a general property
of circles that all rectangles formed from the segments of such intersecting straight lines are equal, that is, the rectangle with base *AE* and
height *EC* is equal in area to the rectangle with base *BE* and height
*ED*.[7] Spinoza contends that in any circle

there are contained infinitely many rectangles equal to one another, though none can be said to exist except insofar as the circle exists; nor can the idea of any of these rectangles exist except insofar as it is comprehended in the idea of the circle. Of these infinitely many rectangles, let two only [that constructed out of *AE* and *EC* and that constructed out of *BE* and *ED*] be conceived to exist. The ideas of these two rectangles also now exist not merely insofar as they are comprehended in the idea of the circle, but also insofar as they involve the existence of those rectangles. By this they are distinguished from the remaining ideas of the remaining rectangles.

The view here seems to be this. Once a particular circle is given, it defines a certain class of rectangles which could be constructed out of the segments of lines intersecting within it. For example, the square of its radius places an upper limit on the area of such rectangles. These will not all be equal in area. But if we take any one point within the circumference of the circle as the point of intersection, this point will define a still narrower class of possible rectangles, all of which will be equal in area. The circle, we may say, contains these rectangles implicitly, in that the possibility of their construction is implied by the nature of the circle. This possibility is actualized whenever someone draws two intersecting lines within the circle, though, of course, there are infinitely many different ways in which it might be actualized. That is, there are infinitely many lines which could be drawn through the point of intersection, each of which would generate a rectangle equal in area to, but of different dimensions than, the existing rectangles. The existence of the undrawn rectangles as implicit in the existence of the circle is analogous to the nondurational existence of the ideas of nonexistent modes as comprehended in the infinite idea of God. The existence of the drawn rectangles is analogous to the durational existence of the ideas of things actually existing.

Such is the example Spinoza gives. And though its point may not be readily apparent, still, if we translate it into the language I have been using, it seems to me that we arrive at an intelligible view. Suppose that we understand by the "infinite idea of God" the laws of nature.

Just as the circle defines a class of possible rectangles, so the laws of nature define classes of possible entities. Given the law of inertia, a body which is not acted on by an external force, but which nevertheless is accelerated, is an impossibility; by contrast, a body not acted on by an external force and moving uniformly in a straight line is a possible entity. In the formal mode, this is to say that the proposition

> ( 1 ) Body *a* is not acted on by an external force, but is accelerating,

is inconsistent with the law of inertia, though not internally inconsistent, whereas

> ( 2 ) Body *a* is not acted on by an external force and is moving uniformly in a straight line

is both internally consistent and consistent with the law of inertia. Whether or not a particular body satisfying the conditions described in ( 2 ) actually exists will, of course, depend on considerations extraneous to scientific theory, just as the actual existence of one of the infinitely many rectangles contained implicitly in the circle will depend on considerations extraneous to geometry. It is only possible existence which is implied by the laws of nature.

I think it very likely that this is the kind of doctrine Spinoza had in mind. But I doubt that he would have wanted to express it in these terms. For he does not seem to want to draw the contrast between durational and eternal existence as a contrast between actual and possible existence. For him, it is rather a contrast between two different kinds of actual existence. Thus he writes in the *Ethics,*

> Things are conceived by us as actual in two ways, either insofar as we conceive them to exist with relation to a particular time and place, or insofar as we conceive them to be contained in God, and to follow from the necessity of the divine nature. But those things which are conceived in this second way as true or real we conceive under the form of eternity. (*E* Vp29s)

I would suggest that Spinoza speaks here of a kind of actual existence, and not merely of possible existence, because he thinks of nonexistent-but-possible entities as being contained implicitly in something which itself actually and eternally exists. (This is one respect in which the analogy with the circle is inadequate—the circle does not exist eternally.) And he will, therefore, call the ideas of such things "true," even though the things themselves never exist at any particular time or in any particular place:

> If an architect conceives a building properly [*ordine*], though such a building may never have existed, and may never exist, nevertheless the thought is true; and the thought remains the same, whether the building exists or not. (*TdIE*, 69, II:26)

The use of the term "true" here strikes us as paradoxical, for it seems to be cut off from the usual requirement of correspondence with reality. But I suspect Spinoza might insist that, just as the thought remains the same, so, in a sense, the building remains the same, whether it exists at a particular time and place or not. For just as the idea of the building is comprehended in the infinite idea of God, so the essence of the building is contained eternally in the attributes of God (*E* IIp8c).

To say this is to imply that even the human body is not absolutely destroyed in death, that something of it too remains which is eternal, that the parallelism of the attributes which seemed to be threatened by the doctrine of the eternity of the mind is, after all, maintained. And many will feel this to be an objection, on the ground that, in Spinoza, only the mind is explicitly stated to be eternal. But this is a rather dubious argument from silence. For to the extent that Spinoza justifies his doctrine of the eternity of the mind by an appeal to *E* IIp8, he does commit himself to saying that what holds of the mind holds equally well of the body. I fail to see why he should have thought himself required to be any more explicit than in fact he is.

A more serious objection, I think, is this: Spinoza speaks only of

a part of the mind as being eternal; if he were thinking of the ideas
of things as being contained in the idea of God in the manner that
I have suggested, then there would be no reason for him to state his
doctrine in this limited way. For if the description of a particular building, say, is consistent with the laws of nature, so that the infinite idea
of God contains the idea of that building, then the whole idea of the
building is contained in the idea of God, not just a part of it. Moreover, later in part V of the *Ethics*, the doctrine of the eternity of the
mind is connected with knowledge of the second and third kinds and
with the aptitude of the body to do many things. There ($E$ Vp38 and
39) Spinoza says that the more the mind understands things by the
second and third kind of knowledge and the more the body is fit for
many things, the greater will be the part of the mind which is eternal.
The apparent implication is that a person could increase the portion of
his mind which is eternal by coming to understand more and more
things *sub specie aeternitatis* and (Heaven help us!) by improving the
fitness of his body.

These passages would not present a problem if Spinoza had said
merely that, as our knowledge of our bodies *sub specie aeternitatis* increases, so also our consciousness of the eternity of the mind increases.
To conceive a thing *sub specie aeternitatis* is to conceive it insofar as
it is conceived through the essence of God ($E$ Vp30D), that is, to see
it as contained in an attribute of God and explicable in terms of the
laws of that attribute. To the extent, then, that we come to understand
a particular state of affairs as an actualization of a possibility perma-
nently embodied in the "fixed and eternal things," we view the idea
of that state of affairs as contained in the idea of God. If the state of
affairs is one involving a part of our body, the idea of that state
of affairs will be one of the ideas constituting our mind, and we shall
have become conscious of a portion of our mind as something eternal.
But Spinoza's language suggests that an increase in our understanding
involves, not merely an increase in our consciousness of the eternity
of the mind, but an increase in the eternity of the mind itself. And
this is a doctrine which, at present, I find completely unintelligible.

## Of the Unknown Attributes of God

Spinoza tells us a fair amount about the attribute of extension, rather less about the attribute of thought, and next to nothing about the infinitely many other attributes of God. No doubt this is as it should be, since he holds that they are at least unknown, and probably unknowable.[8] But it is frustrating. For it means that whatever we may say in an attempt to understand what Spinoza intends by this doctrine, and why he believes it, must be more than usually speculative. Nonetheless, I think it may prove possible to say something useful on the subject.

We begin by considering an analogy put forward by Brunschvicg. The relation between substance and its attributes, he says, may best be understood in the following way:

> A thought, in itself one and indivisible, may be expressed with complete exactness in an infinity of languages. One could say with equal justice that no one of the translations contains the thought and that they all manifest it in its entirety. Just as there is a perfect parallelism between the different texts which express one and the same thought, so also there is an intimate and perpetual correspondence between the different attributes which proceed from one unique activity. Ultimately, from the point of view of absolute reality, all these attributes are only one and the same thing.[9]

This is, as an analogy should be, very suggestive.[10] But perhaps it can be improved upon. I have been supposing, throughout this book, that it makes sense to talk about a *complete* description of the world considered as a system of extended objects. Now suppose we had an alternative description of the world, equally complete, and different not merely in its terminology, but in its conceptual framework.[11] What I have in mind is the kind of "rearrangement of facts" that Erik Stenius describes in his book on Wittgenstein's *Tractatus:*

> It holds good even of our knowledge of the world that "the facts as a whole" can be analysed in different ways. Revolutionary advances in science have, in effect, been connected with a "re-

structuring" of facts applying to the world . . . [An] example is
the new way in which Faraday looked at the facts of electricity.
Faraday, so to speak, regarded the things of his theory not as
"particles of electricity," as was the classical conception, but as
the electrical field lying between the charged objects, and instead
of the mutual attraction and repulsion of the particles, he introduced the tension of the field. What Faraday made was only a
rearrangement of facts already known; he described them in a
new way.[12]

Suppose we had a complete description of the world in terms of mechani-
cal concepts and another in terms of field concepts. This, I take it,
would be the sort of thing that Spinzola's doctrine of the unknown attributes asserts as being possible in principle. The two descriptions would
have certain things in common. The propositions would divide into general and singular, the general propositions into nomological and nonnomological, and the nomological ones would, in each case, be organized
into a deductive system. Each attribute would have an absolute nature
and infinite and finite modes falling under that nature. The descriptions
would differ, however, in the kinds of things and properties which would
be the elements of the facts described by the propositions. Since the
conceptual structures are entirely different, no proposition in one description could be the denial of a proposition in another.

I am uncertain whether this situation is coherently describable. It
might be argued that where in the sciences we have two quite different
accounts of the same thing, say the phenomena of electricity, the two
accounts share a common observational vocabulary, and differ only in
the theoretical superstructure. Indeed, it seems that they must have some
terms in common if, in any intelligible sense, they are about the same
thing. But this is the kind of doubt which, for our purposes, is best
noted and then passed by.

There is one curious consequence of this approach to the unknown
attributes. Given what we have said in the preceding section about
the relation of thought to extension, it implies that the attribute of
thought has a peculiar status. Each alternative description of the world

will generate, not one, but a pair of attributes. For every time we re-construct the facts which make up the totality of facts, we get a new set of propositions corresponding to those facts.

The result is that we shall have to say either ( 1 ) that the attribute of thought is coextensive with all of the other attributes combined, or ( 2 ) that just as there is an attribute of thought corresponding to the attribute of extension, so there are infinitely many other attributes of thought corresponding to some one of the other unknown attributes. These two possibilities may be represented in the following way:

$$
(1)\ \text{substance} \left\{
\begin{array}{l}
\text{extension} \\
X \\
Y \\
Z, \text{etc.}
\end{array}
\right\} \quad \text{thought}
$$

$$
(2)\ \text{substance} \left\{
\begin{array}{l}
\text{extension} \\
\text{thought}_e \\
\\
X \\
\text{thought}_x \\
\\
Y \\
\text{thought}_y, \text{etc.}
\end{array}
\right.
$$

Neither of these pictures is the one we should expect, which looks more like this:

$$
(3)\ \text{substance} \left\{
\begin{array}{l}
\text{extension} \\
\text{thought} \\
\\
X \\
Y \\
Z, \text{etc.}
\end{array}
\right.
$$

Diagrams (1) and (2) give thought a peculiar position among the attributes; (3) puts it on a par with them.

It is worth noting that we could accept the general framework of Chapters 2 and 3, and of this section of Chapter 4, and still accord thought the same status as the other attributes. If we were to follow the suggestion made and rejected at the beginning of this chapter, we could imagine a systematic psychology comparable to the systematic physics we have talked about, with basic psychological laws, derived laws, and predictions of individual thoughts based on those laws. None of the most distinctive features of our interpretation would have to be sacrificed. It is the account of the relation of thought to extension given in the first section of this chapter that forces us to this conclusion.

It would appear, at first glance, to be an unwelcome conclusion. Nevertheless, I should maintain that, if we examine carefully the little evidence we have, we shall find that this consequence of our interpretation is a virtue, not a defect.

Fortunately, the question of the unknown attributes was raised in the three-cornered correspondence which Spinoza participated in with G. H. Schuller and E. W. Tschirnhaus. We find the first mention of difficulty in a letter sent by Schuller to Spinoza on behalf of Tschirnhaus, who had asked Spinoza whether he could give a demonstrative (*ostensiva*) proof, and not one by reduction to absurdity, of the doctrine that

> We cannot know more attributes of God than thought and extension; and further, whether it follows from this that creatures consisting of other attributes, on the other hand, can conceive no extension, and thus would seem to constitute as many worlds as there are attributes of God; for example, our world of extension, as I say, exists and has such and such an extent; so also would the worlds which compose the other attributes exist and have the same extent; and just as we perceive nothing beyond extension except thought, so the creatures of those worlds would have to perceive nothing but the attribute of their world, *and thought*. (*Ep.* 63, IV:275)

Now I think that Tschirnhaus must have understood Spinoza rather well on this point. In his reply (*Ep.* 64, IV:277–278) to the question whether there are not as many worlds as there are attributes[13] Spinoza merely refers Tschirnhaus to *E* IIP7s, according to which "extended substance and thinking substance are one and the same substance, now comprehended under one attribute, now under another." So we may take it that there is only one world, which is now understood in one way, now in another. But Spinoza does not reject anything else Tschirnhaus says, even though there is already a suggestion here that thought may have a special position among the attributes. The greater part of the letter is taken up with providing the requested proof that the human mind can know no other attributes of God beyond thought and extension.

Tschirnhaus is not satisfied. In his next letter, he returns to the attack, asking again for a proof that the mind can perceive no other attributes; for, though he sees clearly enough that this is so, he also thinks that he can demonstrate the contrary from *E* IIP7s. He then purports to set up the deduction, and asks Spinoza to show him where he has misunderstood the sense of the scholium:

> Although I gather from the scholium that the world is certainly unique, nevertheless it is no less clear from that scholium that it is expressed in infinite ways. From this it seems to follow that the modification which constitutes my mind, and the modification which expresses my body, although it is one and the same modification, is nevertheless expressed in infinite ways—in one way through thought, in another through extension, in a third through an attribute of God unknown to me, so on to infinity. For there are infinite attributes of God, and the order and connection of modifications seems to be the same in all. (*Ep.* 65, IV:279)

So far there does not seem to be much that Spinoza could take exception to. But now Tschirnhaus goes on to ask:

> Why the mind, which represents a certain modification, the same

modification being expressed not only in extension but in infinite
other ways, perceives only that modification expressed through extension, that is, the human body, and no other expression through
other attributes.

Historians of philosophy have generally felt that Tschirnhaus has a good
question here. Granted that Spinoza's proof of the mind's confinement
to thought and extension seems to run smoothly enough, and granted
that Tschirnhaus has hardly demonstrated the contrary, nevertheless,
his final query seems a pertinent one. Spinoza's answer is maddeningly
brief, and has widely been regarded as unsatisfactory:

> I say that although each thing is expressed in infinite ways in
> the infinite intellect of God, nevertheless, those infinite ideas by which
> it is expressed cannot constitute one and the same mind of a singular
> thing, but infinitely many minds. For each of the infinitely many
> ideas has no connection with any other, as I have explained in
> *E* IIP7S and is obvious from *E* IP10. If you give your attention
> to these briefly, you will see that there is no longer any difficulty.
> (*Ep.* 66, IV:280)

It is unfortunate that Spinoza took such an optimistic view of his cor-
respondent's acuteness. Later Tschirnhaus complains, through Schuller,
that "by this argument the attribute of thought is made to extend itself
much more widely than the rest of the attributes," though this seems
inconsistent with the doctrine that each of the attributes constitutes the
essence of substance (*Ep.* 70, IV:302). But Spinoza has said his last
word on the subject.

Now what are we to conclude from all of this? First, I think we
may say that the attribute of thought does extend more widely than
any of the others. There is evidently a mode of the attribute of thought,
or a mode of an attribute of thought, for every mode of every one of
the other attributes. This is stated quite explicitly in the *Short Treatise:*

> Therefore the essence of the soul consists only in the existence

> of an idea, or objective essence in the attribute of thought, originat-
> ing from the essence of an object which in fact really exists in
> nature. I say "of an object which really exists" without further
> specification in order to include here not only the modes of exten-
> sion, but also the modes of all the infinite attributes, which have
> a soul just as extension does. (*KV*, appendix, I:119)

The same view that Spinoza put forward in answer to the criticisms
of Tschirnhaus had been expressed clearly in his earliest work—though
it would take a perceptive reader to see it in the *Ethics*.

Secondly, since Spinoza says there is no connection between the idea
of a thing in the attribute of extension and the idea of the same thing
considered under some one of the unkown attributes, it might be better
to represent his thought here by diagram (2) rather than (1). He seems
to think that there are an infinite number of self-contained systems of
ideas.

And finally, it might be suggested[14] that the peculiar status thus given
to thought is implied in the very definition of attribute as "that which
the intellect perceives as constituting the essence of substance" (*E* IA4).
The intellect mentioned here is later referred to as an infinite intellect
(*E* IIP7S). If it is to perceive all the attributes of substance and there
are infinitely many of those attributes, then it must be what Spinoza
would call absolutely infinite, and not merely infinite in its kind (*E* ID2).
And since an attribute is defined as something which this intellect
perceives, there could hardly be an attribute which the intellect failed
to perceive.

So I think we may say that the special status which our interpretation
accords to the attribute of thought is not a difficulty. On the contrary,
it is a requirement of any adequate interpretation that it account in
some way for the undeniable fact that thought does have a special position among the attributes.

Still, I should not wish my hypothesis of the possibility of alternative
complete descriptions of the world to be taken as anything more than

a very tentative suggestion. It is, necessarily, founded on very little evidence. Some of its implications are right, but others are not. For example, there is nothing in the hypothesis to explain why the infinite unknown attributes should be unknowable. The possibility of alternative scientific accounts of the same phenomena was a live one for Spinoza and his contemporaries—Galileo's *Dialogues on the Two Chief Systems of the World* were published in 1632, the year of Spinoza's birth. My hypothesis would accord better with the contrary view, that the unknown attributes are knowable. But it is clear that the mature Spinoza would not accept this.

Putting aside the problem of what is involved in Spinoza's assertion of infinitely many unknowable attributes, there remains the question: "Why did he define God as a substance consisting of infinite attributes?"—a question which Seligman has posed as a difficult one for any naturalistic interpretation.

In a way, the answer to this is easy. Spinoza's definition of God, like most of his definitions of key terms, is presented as a stipulative definition, an explanation of the meaning he attaches to the term in his work. "By God, *I* understand . . ." But Spinoza's stipulations are rarely arbitrary, they generally preserve some continuity with existing philosophical usage. Since there is clearly ample precedent for the definition of God (cf. Wolfson, I, 118), the fact that Spinoza defines God in this way poses no real problem, for a naturalistic interpretation or for any other.

The real problem—and it is a problem that is particularly acute for a naturalistic interpretation—is to understand why Spinoza should have thought that Nature must have infinitely many attributes. To conceive God as a being absolutely infinite is quite traditional; to conceive Nature as a being absolutely infinite is revolutionary. The naturalistic interpreter, who wishes to read the equation "God = Nature" with the emphasis on "Nature," has some explaining to do.

We can, of course, turn to the argument Spinoza offers us in various places. The major premise is that

(1) The more being or reality a thing has,
the more attributes it has (*E* I$p$9).

In the demonstration Spinoza claims that this is evident from the definition of "attribute." Elsewhere he is more enlightening. Following Descartes, he rejects the possibility of a vacuum on the ground that nothing,
that is, nonbeing, what does not exist, can have no properties
(*Ep.* 13, IV:65). Conversely, to be, or to be real, is to have properties—
as Spinoza puts it, each being must be conceived under some attribute
(*Ep.* 9, *E* I$p$10s). From this Spinoza thinks it follows that the more
being or reality a thing has, the more attributes it has, and that

(2) The most real being, the *ens realissimum*,
must have infinitely many attributes.

This is nowhere asserted explicitly, but it appears to be presupposed.
To get from this to the conclusion that Nature has infinitely many attributes, we would need the further premise that

(3) Nature is the *ens realissimum*.

The question then would be what reason there is for asserting this.

It is not too difficult to find a possible reason. Remembering that
Spinoza identifies reality with perfection (*E* II$d$6) and perfection with
power (*E* IV pref.), we might argue that the omnipotence of Nature,
the status of *Natura naturans* as the necessarily existing, uncaused first
cause of all things is a sufficient ground both for calling it the *ens realissimum* and for concluding that it must have infinitely many attributes.

But while this argument may, after a fashion, be intelligible, it does
not seem to me to provide any real understanding. It smacks too much
of verbal manipulation. And I suggest that the difficulty in understanding Spinoza on this point arises from the fact that here he is trying
to articulate an intuitive feeling which resists clear expression. In the
*Short Treatise* he writes:

> After the preceding consideration of Nature, we have so far been
> able to find in it only two attributes which belong to this all-perfect
> being. And these attributes give us nothing to satisfy us that they

are the only ones which constitute this perfect being—on the contrary, we find in ourselves something which openly proclaims to us the existence, not merely of a great many, but of infinitely many perfect attributes, which must belong to this perfect being before it can be said to be perfect. And where does this idea of perfection come from? This something . . . can only come from the infinite attributes themselves, which tell us that they are, but not what they are. (*KV*, I, i, I:17)

It is possible that we owe this "formless vision of unseen worlds"[15] to the scientific developments of Spinoza's time. The discoveries of the telescope and the microscope had a very considerable effect on the seventeenth-century imagination. For they demonstrated forcefully that, to beings operating with different perceptual equipment, our familiar world would look altogether different. Something of this fascination with the effects of changed conditions of perception is reflected in much of the literature of the time, Swift's *Gulliver's Travels* being the best known example.[16] Spinoza himself displays it when he writes to Oldenburg about how the world might seem to a tiny worm living in the blood (*Ep.* 32). I should not wish to press this sort of speculation too far. The worm, after all, no matter how small, is still a mode of extension. The point is simply that considerations of this kind *may* have inspired in Spinoza the feeling that the world must be capable of being understood in infinitely many different ways, and that this feeling *may* then have found philosophical expression in the doctrine of the infinite attributes and dubious support in the unconvincing argument outlined earlier.

At any rate, whatever may have been the philosophical motivation for thinking that Nature must have infinite attributes, this doctrine certainly did much to justify Spinoza's identification of God and Nature. For, as he was to point out himself to Oldenburg (*Ep.* 73, IV:307), that identification did not involve the equation of God with "a certain mass or corporeal matter." On the contrary, it assumed a conception of Nature as being, in its own right, absolutely infinite. Provided that we follow Spinoza in his conception of Nature, I think there is no reason to object to the equation.

Spinoza's philosophy consists mainly in the negation of the double dualism between God and the world and between soul and body which his teacher Descartes had set up.

—Schopenhauer, *The Fourfold Root of the Principle of Sufficient Reason*

# Postscript

F. H. Jacobi once said that no one to whom a single line of the *Ethics* remained dark could claim to have understood Spinoza. By that standard, it may be doubted whether any one has ever understood Spinoza, including Spinoza himself. But by any reasonable standard, I think we can claim to have made some progress toward an understanding.

Admittedly, those who have gone to Spinoza expecting to find "the strife of conflicting systems" have found, generally, the strife of conflicting systems. Those who have sought a grand synthesis of the Greek, Jewish, and Christian traditions have discovered, not too surprisingly, a Spinoza rightly called "the last of the medievals." It was, perhaps, inevitable that I, who have looked in Spinoza for a system that would appear coherent and plausible to me, should, on the whole, have succeeded in locating one.

Such reflections must have a sobering effect on any would-be interpreter of Spinoza. But without wishing to maintain that only my portrait gives a good likeness, I would still insist that it *is* a good likeness, that my emphasis on explanation in terms of natural law is fundamentally rightheaded, and that anyone disposed to differ with me should ask himself how he would deal with the passages I have cited.

Before surrendering this work finally to the critics' knives, however, there is one quite general objection I should like to anticipate. My account of Spinoza tends to suggest that he was primarily a metaphysician with an interest in philosophy of science, whose views happened to have consequences for ethics, whereas Spinoza's writings and the titles of his major works suggest rather that his concern with ethics was primary and his interest in metaphysics secondary. To ignore the moral convictions that underlay the metaphysics is to leave out of account what mattered most to Spinoza.

This note is often sounded in the literature on Spinoza—and no doubt rightly. It is certainly true, as the autobiographical passages at the beginning of the *Treatise* show, that Spinoza's interest in philosophy was very largely the result of ethical concerns. In this early work he describes movingly how his disillusionment with the worldly goods of

Fame, Wealth, and Sensual Pleasure led him to search for a more worthy object of his love, to look beyond the world of change for something eternal. Plainly, this philosophical mood accounts for a great deal of what we find in the *Ethics*. A book on Spinoza—even a book restricted to his metaphysics—which ignores altogether this aspect of his thought is bound to give a somewhat misleading impression.

Still, there are two things that we need to remember. The first is that Spinoza himself would surely have rejected the suggestion that his metaphysical views were dependent on or determined by his ethical views. The order in which he wrote the *Ethics* supports the contrary conclusion: that he regarded the doctrines about God in part I as capable of standing on their own and that he took them to be logically prior to the ethical theses developed in the later parts of that work. Whatever the motives may have been that led him to engage in his curious brand of theology, his philosophical temperament was very far from that which postulates the eternal order to satisfy the demands of practical reason. And the god whose existence he thought demonstrable would have given little consolation to poor old Lampe.

Second—and more important—for the historian trying to understand why Spinoza arrived at *this* ontology rather than some other one, it is not very helpful to be told that he had a lust for the eternal. This will explain, perhaps, why he did not come up with an ontology of the Humean sort, in which the furniture of the world is constructed out of fleeting impressions and ideas. But it will not explain why his Platonism took the peculiar form it did. Nor will it add a great deal to invoke the scientific spirit of the age. Descartes and Leibniz, Locke and Berkeley, all worked in much the same intellectual climate. Each came to terms with the scientific revolution in one way or another. Each made room in his ontology for the eternal in one way or another. But no two of these men did this in the same way. And Spinoza's way was radically different from that of any of them. Why?

I think we may best answer this question by seeing Spinoza's philosophy as a reaction against Descartes. For all that Spinoza owed Descartes—

and he owed him much—the points of difference between the two philosophers offer the best opportunity for reconstructing the development
of the Spinozistic system. There are, of course, many points of difference.
But the most fundamental one, in my view, was that for Spinoza the
world was thoroughly intelligible. As Spinoza had Meyer point out in
his preface to the *Principles of Descartes' Philosophy,* when we read
in that work that

> "this or that exceeds human grasp," we must not suppose that
> the author [Spinoza] is putting this forward as his own opinion.
> For he thinks that all these things, and many others even more
> sublime and subtle, not only can be conceived by us clearly and
> distinctly, but can be explained very easily, provided that, in the
> search for truth and the knowledge of things, the human intellect
> is led by a path different from that opened up by Descartes. (I:132)

If rationalism consists in having this optimistic view of man's ability
to comprehend the world around him, then Spinoza was plainly and
unequivocally a rationalist.

But Descartes was not. In at least two crucial respects he made the
world a mystery—first by exempting man from the domain of law and
setting him up as "a kingdom within a kingdom" (*E* III pref.) whose
actions could only be given a verbal explanation by appeal to the obscure
notion of the human will (*E* V pref.), and second by maintaining that
the eternal truths, the laws of nature, had been set up by God as a
king establishes the laws in his kingdom (Adam and Tannery, I: 145,
cf. *E* IIp3s). Descartes had felt compelled to deny that these eternal
truths could hold independently of the will of God. To do so would
be to cast God as "a Jupiter or Saturn, making him subject to Styx
and the Fates."

With this denial Spinoza agreed (*E* Ip33s2). But he could not accept
the anthropomorphic Cartesian alternative for quite a number of reasons.
To begin with, since acts of will are the sort of thing that take place

at a particular time, it applied a temporal concept to the explanation
of something supposed to be eternal. But more important, it did not
offer a genuine explanation. It postulated God's will as a cause in one
breath, and in the next admitted that this cause could just as easily
have had a contrary effect. To do this is to cloak ignorance in specious
verbiage. A cause from which the effect cannot be inferred is not a
cause. Furthermore, since it was conceded that God could have willed
a different set of laws, there was no good reason to think that he would
not change his mind and alter the eternal order. In the letter to Marin
Mersenne cited above, Descartes argued that this could not happen, on
the ground that God's will was immutable. But as Descartes also denied
that there was any necessary connection between God's nature or essence
and his will as exemplified in the nature of the world he created, it
was difficult to see why his will should not change. As Spinoza remarked,

> if it is permitted to attribute to God another intellect and another
> will without any change in his essence and perfection, what is the
> reason why he cannot now change his decrees about created things
> and nevertheless remain equally perfect? His intellect and will re-
> garding created things and their order would remain the same in
> relation to his essence and perfection no matter how it be con-
> ceived. (*E* Ip33s2, II:75)

The specter of Hume rises before us and we contemplate the possibility
of a world in which nothing is stable and enduring.

Spinoza's way out of this dilemma was to identify the will or intellect
of God, the universal laws of nature, with the essence of God. God
is neither the slave nor the master of eternal truth, he is eternal truth.
The laws of nature neither require nor admit explanation in terms of
anything more ultimate, they could not have been otherwise. This is
the first of the two main tenets of Spinozism; and the second, that
man is a part of nature, following her laws in all his actions, is propounded in the same spirit. Both doctrines arise from the fundamental
demand for absolute intelligibility.

Notes, Index

# Notes

PREFACE

1. Heinrich Heine, *Religion and Philosophy in Germany,* trans. John Snodgrass (Boston: Beacon Press, 1959), p. 80.
2. *The Portable Nietzsche,* ed. Walter Kaufmann (New York: Viking Press, 1954), p. 92.


I THE DEFINITIONS OF SUBSTANCE AND MODE

1. *An Essay Concerning Human Understanding,* ed. A. S. Pringle-Pattison (Oxford: Clarendon Press, 1924), II, 23.
2. Arnauld and Nicole, p. 47.
3. Arnauld and Nicole, p. 47. Their language in this passage may suggest that modes are to be regarded as nonsubstantial particulars which cannot exist apart from their own proper subject, rather than as universals, which, though they must exist in some subject or other, need not exist in any particular subject in order to exist. For they say that they conceive the roundness as "unable to subsist naturally without the body whose roundness it is." But this statement is clarified a bit further on. "It is not that one cannot conceive the mode without paying distinct and explicit attention to its subject; rather what shows that the idea of the relation to the substance is involved at least confusedly in that of the mode is that we cannot deny this relation without destroying the idea we have of the mode . . . for example, I can easily conceive prudence without paying distinct attention to a man who is prudent, but I cannot conceive prudence while denying the relation it has to a man or to another intelligent nature which has that virtue" (p. 48). *The locus classicus* for the notion of inherence is, of course, Aristotle's *Categories,* chap. ii. The same difficulty, less easily resolved, arises there. See *Categories and de Interpretatione,* trans. with notes by J. L. Ackrill (Oxford: Clarendon Press, 1963) and G. E. L. Owen, "Inherence," *Phronesis,* 10:97–105 (1965).
4. Adam and Tannery, IX:47. I have rendered the French version, which is fuller and, it seems to me, clearer than the Latin. The French version in general makes a great many additions to the Latin. Adam thinks that some of these

must have been made by Descartes, others by the French translator; but how many and which ones were made by Descartes is obscure. In any case, Descartes authorized the French version.

5. E.g., in the synopsis of the *Meditations,* Adam and Tannery, IX:10, substance is what cannot exist without being created by God; in the Third Meditation, Adam and Tannery IX:35, substance is that which of itself is capable of existing; in the reply to the Fourth Objections, Adam and Tannery IX:175, substance is what "can exist by itself, i.e., without the aid of any other substance."

6. Adam and Tannery, VII:176, 222. In the latter passage, Descartes makes a distinction analogous to Arnauld's own later distinction between a thing and a qualified thing: "Thus to the first I reply that by a *complete thing* I understand nothing other than a substance clothed with those forms or attributes which suffice for me to recognize from them that it is a substance. For we do not know substances immediately, as is noted elsewhere, but only from this, that we perceive certain forms or attributes, which must exist in something in order to exist, we call that thing in which they exist *substance.*"

7. Brunschvicg, "La Révolution Cartésienne et la notion Spinoziste de la substance," *Revue de Métaphysique et de Morale,* 12:764 (1904).

8. Adam and Tannery, IX:47 (still following the French version). In the Latin, the crucial sentence is obscure: "Verumtamen non potest substantia primum animadverti ex hoc solo, quod sit res existens, quia hoc solum per se nos non afficit." Adam and Tannery, VIII:25. Haldane and Ross render this: "Yet substance cannot be first discovered merely from the fact that it is a thing that exists, for that fact alone does not affect us." *The Philosophical Works of Descartes,* 2 vols. (Cambridge, Eng.: Cambridge University Press, 1911), I, 240.

9. The definition in terms of independent existence ("By substance we understand what requires the concurrence of God alone to exist") is given in *PP*IID2, I:181. The definition of substance as the subject of attributes ("Everything in which there exists immediately, as in a subject, or through which there exists anything which we perceive, that is, any property or quality or attribute, of which there is a real idea in us, is called substance") occurs in *PP*ID5, I:150.

10. Among the critics are R. H. M. Elwes, who in his introduction to the *Chief Works of Spinoza,* 2 vols. (New York: Dover, 1951) dismisses it as "grossly inaccurate," and Paul Vernière, who in *Spinoza et la pensée française avant la Révolution,* 2 vols. (Paris: Presses Universitaires de France, 1954), I, 304 describes it as a "caricature." Among the Enlightenment followers of Bayle are Hume, in the *Treatise of Human Nature,* book I, part IV, chap. 2, and Voltaire, in *Le philosophe ignorant.* It should be pointed out, however, that Hume's use of the Bayle critique had an obvious ulterior motive, and that Voltaire's attitude

toward Bayle's criticisms underwent some development. Whereas Voltaire had written of Spinoza in 1766 that "it would be strange if Bayle had not understood him," he wrote in 1771 that "I have always had a suspicion that Spinoza, with his universal substance, his modes and his accidents, understood something other than what Bayle understood, and that as a result, Bayle may have been right without having refuted Spinoza." See H. T. Mason, *Pierre Bayle and Voltaire* (Oxford: Oxford University Press, 1963), pp. 105–107.

11. See particulary remark DD.

12. Remark N, pp. 309–310. Cf. Russell: "Spinoza's metaphysic is the best example of what may be called 'logical monism'—the doctrine, namely, that the world as a whole is a simple substance, none of whose parts are logically capable of existing alone. The ultimate basis for this view is the belief that every proposition has a single subject and a single predicate, which leads to the conclusion that relations and plurality are illusory" (p. 600). Russell's discussion, however, seems more indebted to Joachim than to Bayle.

13. Remark DD. Bayle may have in mind Burgersdijck's *Institutiones Metaphysicae:* "We divide Being first into substance and accident." "Substance is being subsisting through itself. The phrase 'subsisting through itself' in this definition does not exclude dependence on all causes (for in that sense, only God can be said to subsist through himself) but only dependence on a subject." Cited by Wolfson, I, 63n, 64n. Burgersdijck was a Professor of Philosophy at the University of Leyden in the early part of the seventeenth century. His works were used by both Bayle and Spinoza.

14. *E* Ip8s2, my italics. Notice that in the italicized phrase Spinoza is paraphrasing, not quoting his earlier definition of "substance." The effect of the paraphrase is to establish an equivalence between "being conceived through $X$" and "being known through $X$." Unfortunately this interesting variation is not preserved in the Elwes translation.

15. *Ex vi terminorum.* I am here supposing what will be argued in more detail later.

16. This meets half of Leibniz' demand that Spinoza prove that whatever has one characteristic also has the other. For an argument to show that whatever is conceived through itself must also exist in itself, see below.

17. This meets the other half of Leibniz' demand. Cf. the alternative demonstration of Ip6.

18. See remark DD. I have in mind particularly the passage in which Bayle argues that the principal question is how the term "modification" is to be understood in Spinoza's system: "Must it be taken for the same thing that is commonly called 'created substance' [the usual view] or must it be taken in the sense

it has in Descartes' system? I believe the latter is correct, for in the other sense, Spinoza would have acknowledged creatures distinct from divine substance who have been made either out of nothing or from a matter distinct from God. Now it would be easy to prove from a great number of passages that he admits neither of these two things. Extension, according to him, is an attribute of God. It follows that God is essentially, eternally and necessarily an extended thing, and that extension is as proper to him as existence. From which it follows that the particular varieties of extension, which make up the sun, earth . . . and so on, are in God in the way in which the School philosophers suppose they are in prime matter." I cannot see that this follows. In any case, if it did the argument could end here, for it would have been shown that the particular varieties of extension exist in God as in a subject, which was the point to be proven. Bayle, however, continues: "If these philosophers supposed that prime matter is a simple and perfectly unique substance, they would conclude that the sun and the earth are really the same substance. It must be the case that Spinoza came to the same conclusion. If he did not say that the sun is composed of divine extension, he would have to admit that the sun's extension has been made from nothing." The alternative mentioned originally, that creatures distinct from God might be made from a matter distinct from God, has apparently been forgotten. Bayle goes on: "But he denies creation, and he is therefore obliged to say that the substance of God is the material cause of the sun, is what composes the sun, [*subjectum ex quo,*] and consequently that it is not distinct from God." (Bayle, p. 335. The bracketed phrase is omitted by Popkin.) Spinoza never speaks of God as the material cause of his modes. To the extent that he uses the Aristotelian classification of causes, God is described only as the efficient cause of his modes. See *E*Ip16ci; *KV*I, iii, I:35; *CM*II, x, I:268.

19. Cf. the article "Pyrrho." The ground for holding them false is that they are inconsistent with what is known by religious authority. This is strange itself because one of the self-evident truths thus known to be false is the principle of contradiction.

20. Cf. remark O. Bayle's reply is crudely pragmatic. If Spinozism is no less open to objection than Christianity, then Christianity ought to be preferred because it promises us infinite happiness in the next life.

21. *TdIE*, 101, II:36–37. "The essences of singular mutable things are not to be drawn from their series or order of existence. That would provide us with nothing more than their extrinsic denominations, relations, or at most, circumstances, all of which are far from the inmost essence of things. The essence is really only to be sought solely from fixed and eternal things."

22. There is an interesting passage in Joachim's posthumously published com-

mentary, *Spinoza's Tractatus*, in which he seems to take back much of what he had said in the *Study*. See the discussion of Spinoza's doctrine of essence, pp. 36–44. How far this represents a change of view would be difficult to say.

23. Joachim recognizes this in *Spinoza's Tractatus*. See pp. 60–88, esp. pp. 80–81.

24. Again Joachim's *Spinoza's Tractatus* takes what looks to be a much less extreme position. See pp. 34–35. The same example suggests what Joachim denies, that the content of knowledge need not vary from one kind of knowledge to another. Only the way in which knowledge is arrived at, and consequently the degree of certainty, vary.

25. See e.g., P. H. Nidditch's chapter on Spinoza, in D. J. O'Connor's *Critical History of Western Philosophy* (New York: Free Press, 1964).

26. As Passmore has pointed out in "The Idea of a History of Philosophy," *History and Theory,* Beiheft 5:2–3 (1965), it is necessary, according to Wolfson, to take into account Spinoza's supposed criticisms of his predecessors. This makes the task of finding precedents much easier.

27. There is *some* warrant in Aristotle for identifying an individual with its essence. In the *Metaphysics* Aristotle raises the question "Whether each thing and its essence are the same or different" (1031a15) and concludes that "each primary and self-subsistent thing is one and the same as its essence" (1032a5), principally on the ground that to know a thing is to know its essence. Later, however, this is clarified: "We have stated that the essence and the thing itself are in some cases the same, i.e., in the case of primary substances, e.g., curvature and the essence of curvature, if this is primary. (By a primary substance I mean one which does not imply the presence of something in something else, i.e., in something that underlies it which acts as matter). But things which are of the nature of matter, or of wholes that include matter, are not the same as their essences" (1037a32–1037b7). Aristotle's ground for this is perhaps given in book VII, chap. xv, where he argues that concrete things are indefinable.

28. In one passage (I, 325–328), Wolfson attempts to undercut this objection by arguing that God is an exception to the general rule about universals, since it is an *ens rationis* "only in the sense that its real existence can be discovered only by the mind, by the ontological proofs based upon the adequacy of the idea of God in our mind. In truth, God is an *ens reale*." But he does not really provide any evidence for this claim. The passages he does cite, from the *Short Treatise* and from Aristotle, are quite irrelevant, since they merely point out certain differences between the whole–part relation and the relation of universal to particular.

29. Hallett does not attempt to argue this, except by pointing out that all of Taylor's evidence for equating the relation of substance and mode with that

of subject and predicate comes from Leibniz, not Spinoza.

30. Page 687. "Hume banished the concept of substance from psychology, as Berkeley had banished it from physics."

31. If this is correct, then Spinoza does have a reply to the criticism of G. Dawes Hicks (*Proceedings of the Aristotelian Society,* n.s., 18:337–338 [1917–18]) that the argument for *E* Ip7 (that it pertains to the nature of substance to exist) is a *petitio principii:* "The argument assumes . . . what it purports to establish. For if substance has no cause outside itself, it follows that it must have an inner cause *only* on the assumption that it is existent, and that such existence needs a cause, in accordance with the dictum . . . that 'of any existing thing there must necessarily be some cause on account of which it exists.' "

32. See, e.g., Hamphsire, "There can only be one substance so defined [as *causa sui*], and nothing can exist independently of, or distinct from, this single substance; everything which exists must be conceived as an attribute or modification of, or as in some way inherent in, this single substance; this substance is therefore to be identified with Nature conceived as a whole or as the totality of things" (p. 31).

33. Since arriving at this conclusion I find that Paul Seligman has reached it by a different route. See "Some Aspects of Spinozism," *Proceedings of the Aristotelian Society,* n.s., 61:121 (1960–61). He cites a concurring passage from Wolfson (I, 324ff).

2 THE CAUSALITY OF GOD

1. See, e.g., Joachim, *Study,* pp. 99ff and 120, and Caird, passim.

2. I think Albert Rivaud is right in supposing that in the axioms and lemmas following *E* IIp13 we have a sketch of a work on physics which Spinoza projected but never finished. See "La Physique de Spinoza," *Chronicon Spinozanum,* 4:24–57 (1924–26).

3. "Animadversiones ad Joh. George Wachteri librum de recondita Hebraeorum philosophia," Wiener, p. 497. On the history of this work see Friedman, pp. 155–178. Cf. Gerhardt, I:148.

4. These definitions are not given by Spinoza himself, but are derived from Burgersdijck's *Logic,* whose classification of causes Spinoza followed. See Wolf, pp. 190–195.

5. There is, as Professor Passmore has reminded me, a sense in which Hume does not deny necessary connections either, but merely explains them away psychologically.

6. Of course most people who have rejected the reduction of general propositions to truth-functions of singular ones have not followed Russell in admitting general facts, but have sought a way out through some form of instrumentalist conception of general propositions.

7. "Metaphysics and Ethics," in *The Nature of Metaphysics,* ed. D. F. Pears (London: Macmillan 1957).

8. Spinoza's first published work was an axiomatic presentation of the first two parts of Descartes' *Principles of Philosophy*. It is well known that he ground lenses for a living and that he had acquired a sufficient reputation in optics that people were frequently referred to him (for example, Leibniz). One fruit of this work was his *Treatise on the Rainbow*. His correspondence shows him keeping in touch with the activities of the newly formed Royal Society through its first secretary, Henry Oldenburg. He was particularly interested in Robert Boyle's work in chemistry.

9. I have in mind Ralph M. Blake's excellent study, "The Role of Experience in Descartes' Theory of Method," which originally appeared in the *Philosophical Review*, 38:125–143, 201–218 (1929), and has since been reprinted in *Theories of Scientific Method: The Renaissance through the Nineteenth Century,* ed. Edward H. Madden (Seattle: University of Washington Press, 1960).

10. See, e.g., Morris Cohen, "Amor Dei Intellectualis," *Chronicon Spinozanum,* III:3–19 (1923). Similar remarks apply to my emphasis on explanation in terms of causal laws (see Harald Höffding, "Das Erste Buch der Ethica," *Chronicon Spinozanum,* II:20–53 [1922]) and my emphasis on the ideal of the unity of science (see Hampshire's *Spinoza*).

11. "Some Aspects of Spinozism," *Proceedings of the Aristotelian Society,* 61:109–128 (1960–61).


3 NECESSITY

1. The interpretation of Leibniz on the topic of necessary truth and on related topics has considerable difficulties of its own that I do not wish to get too deeply involved in here. It will suffice for my purposes if the views I attribute to Leibniz represent a plausible reading of the texts. My account is drawn mainly from the *Discourse on Metaphysics,* Gerhardt, IV:427–463, and two short papers in Louis Couturat, *Opuscules et fragments inédits de Leibniz* (Paris: Presses Universitaires de France, 1903), pp. 16–22 and 518–523.

2. By "analytic" I understand here a proposition whose truth or falsity may be determined by reduction to a logical truth or logical falsehood through the

substitution of definitions for definable terms. For a discussion of definition, see below.

3. I owe this point to Mr. Loren Lomasky who makes it, not against Leibniz, but against P. F. Stawson's version of Leibniz, in an unpublished paper, "Strawson and the Identity of Indiscernibles." He would not charge Leibniz with a vicious regress, since he does not think that, for Leibniz, relational predicates are included in the concept of an individual. I am not certain that he is right on this point, but it is an obscure one. Leibniz certainly mentions relational predicates in some of his expositions of the theory of individual concepts (cf. the *Discourse on Metaphysics,* section 8, where he includes "will conquer Darius and Porus" in the individual concept of Alexander). No doubt he had hopes of reducing these relational predicates to nonrelational ones, but it is difficult to say precisely what his intentions were, or how far he was or could be successful in carrying them out. I think it would be very difficult to make any sense of the doctrine that each individual substance expresses the whole universe except on the supposition that some sort of relational predicates are included in the individual concept.

4. Cf. Gerhardt, VII:356. To find a consistent account of the principle in Leibniz is notoriously difficult. See Lovejoy, pp. 145–146, and George Parkinson, *Logic and Reality in Leibniz's Metaphysics* (London: Oxford University Press, 1965), pp. 56–75.

5. However, the claim that existential propositions are not generally analytic looks rather arbitrary. Leibniz justifies his doctrine of individual concepts by an appeal to the nature or definition of truth. A true proposition simply is one in which the concept of the subject includes the concept of the predicate. If so, why are most existential propositions an exception? The only answer that suggests itself is that existence is not a predicate. But Leibniz will hardly wish to say that because he treats existence as a predicate in the ontological argument.

6. Lovejoy appears to deny this: "Spinoza . . . thus expressed the principle of plenitude [roughly, whatever is logically possible exists] in its most uncompromising form and . . . represented it as necessary in the strict logical sense. Everything shared in the same completely sufficient reason for being that the existence of God was by most philosophers conceived to possess" (p. 155). This suggests that all true existential propositions are absolutely necessary.

In other places Lovejoy is more cautious: "The other argument for the existence of God is the argument from the necessity of the existence of anything whose existence is not precluded by *some* logical impossibility" (p. 153, my italics). Lovejoy seems here to recognize that the nonexistence of things that exist (God excepted) must be logically impossible in some sense other than absolute logical impossibility.

7. Cf. the discussion of fictions in the *Treatise, TdIE,* 52–58, II : 19–22.

8. I should point out, however, that the notion of an accidental generalization, as I am using it, is broader than Popper's notion of a numerically universal statement. My accidental generalizations include existential generalizations.

9. I write "general" in this paragraph, though accuracy would require "universal." My reason is that the questions (1) are universal generalizations reducible to truth-functions of singular propositions? and (2) are existential generalizations reducible to truth-functions of singular propositions? are commonly treated as though they would necessarily have the same answer. But it is not clear to me that they would. For though it may be the case that no singular proposition or truth-function of singular propositions ever entails a universal generalization, it is surely not the case that no singular proposition ever entails an existential generalization. If existential generalizations are not "reducible" to singular propositions it must be because they are logically weaker, not logically stronger, than singular propositions. "Jones is a man" does entail "There are men," though "There are men" does not entail any singular proposition or truth-function thereof. This is a bit curious and shows just how obscure the notion of reducibility is. I have been proceeding on the assumption that logical equivalence is necessary and probably sufficient for reducibility. I do not think "reducible" has always been used that way. Russell, when he wrote *The Philosophy of Logical Atomism,* thought there were no disjunctive facts, though he thought we had to admit existence facts. But surely disjunctive propositions stand in the same relation to singular ones that existential propositions do to singular propositions and truth-functions thereof—they are logically weaker, not logically equivalent.

10. I have borrowed the example from Willam Kneale, *Probability and Induction* (London: Oxford University Press, 1949), pp. 29–30. I take it that I am also expounding his view of the matter and that he, in turn, is providing a rationale for the cryptic passage (in section 23 of *The Logic of Scientific Discovery,* London: Hutchinson, 1959, originally published in Vienna in 1934 as *Logik der Forschung*) in which Popper puts forward the thesis here discussed. Popper takes no account of the Russellian criticism of the reducibility thesis.

In answer to the objection that, when the region is large, it will be impossible to "take in the whole at once," Kneale replies that we can "work out a scheme for dividing the whole into an exhaustive set of parts each of which can be inspected in turn." The statement about the whole would be equivalent to a conjunction of statements about its parts. Presumably there would be no need for a further conjunct to the effect that *a, b, c, d,* etc. are *all* the parts of the whole. For if the division is systematic, this statement could be argued to be analytic.

My difficulty with Kneale lies in his claim that "The use of the word 'all'
in restricted universal statements of the type we have been considering can therefore
be explained by reference to its use in the singular in such totality statements
as 'The building is all stone' or 'Africa is all hot,' but the use of the word
in what I call totality statements is primitive and does not *admit or require*
explanation by reference to any other use" (my italics). I can see why someone
might wish to say that "The buildng is all stone" does not *have* to be transformed
into "All parts of the building are stone." But I cannot see why it *may* not
be. Hence my hesitation in the text over whether to write "can be regarded"
or "is properly regarded."

11. *Two New Sciences,* trans. H. Crew and A. de Salvio (New York: Dover,
1914), pp. 162–164.

12. See Gerald J. Holton, *Introduction to Concepts and Theories in Physical
Science* (Reading, Mass.: Addison-Wesley, 1952), pp. 318–319. Cf. *Two New
Sciences,* pp. 62–63, 276, 290–291. There is an extremely interesting discussion
of Galileo's methodology in Ludovico Geymonat, *Galileo Galilei* (New York:
McGraw-Hill, 1965).

13. See A. Rupert Hall, *From Galileo to Newton, 1630–1720* (New York:
Harper and Row, 1963), p. 38.

14. This was the remark which prompted de Vries to ask whether things or
their affections were eternal truths. Cf. above, p. 89 and *Ep.* 10, IV:47.

15. "Definition and Its Problems" *Philosophical Review,* 52:566 (1943).

16. Cf. Richard Robinson, *Definition* (London: Oxford University Press, 1950),
pp. 161–165. I am very much indebted to Robinson's whole discussion of definition.

17. *The Logic of Scientific Discovery,* p. 431.

## 4 THE DIVINE ATTRIBUTES

1. I had originally added the name of Hume to those of Descartes and Locke,
but Professor Passmore has reminded me that, in view of Hume's theory of
belief, this would not be correct. The similarity between Hume and Spinoza
on this point is not doubt connected with the fact that they both adopt no-substance
theories of the mind. Just as, for Hume, the mind is nothing but a bundle
or collection of perceptions, so for Spinoza the mind is entirely constituted by
its ideas.

2. "Fact" also causes some embarrassment for Britan when he gets down to
*narratio falsa, quae erat facti, quod nullibi contigerat.* Cf. *The Principles of
Descartes' Philosophy* (Chicago: Open Court, 1905), p. 132.

3. My debt here is to C. A. Baylis ("Facts, Propositions, Exemplification,

and Truth," *Mind*, 67:459–479 [1948] and C. I. Lewis, *An Analysis of Knowledge and Valuation* (Lasalle, Ill.: Open Court, 1946). But they are not to be held responsible for the use I make of their ideas.

4. My example is constructed on the analogy of one of Donald Davidson's in "Actions, Reasons and Causes," *Journal of Philosophy*, 60:686 (1963). Davidson writes "I flip the switch, turn on the light and illuminate the room. Unbeknownst to me I also alert a prowler to the fact that I am home. Here I do not do four things, but only one, of which four descriptions have been given." I suppose that what applies to actions applies, *mutatis mutandis*, to facts. For a variety of cases, some of which seem to me more difficult, see Romane Clark, "Facts," *Southern Journal of Philosophy*, 21:123–136 (1966).

5. Cf. Joachim, *Spinoza's Tractatus*, p. 90: there are "two notoriously difficult questions" in Spinoza's epistemology— "(1) in what precise sense, according to Spinoza, we know our body, and (2) how, on the other hand, a mind, which is the *essentia objectiva* of our body, can be (or have) knowledge of anything besides."

6. Or that the fact which *p* describes involves Peter's nature. Spinoza speaks both of bodily modifications and of their ideas as "involving" the nature of external bodies.

7. This is theorem 35 in book III of Euclid's *Elements*. I have given a somewhat different exposition of the example than Spinoza does, but I think it is faithful to his intentions. I should mention that in the interpretation of this scholium I am very much indebted to Mr. A. J. Watt, whose "The Divine Intellect and Will in the *Ethics* of Spinoza," an M. A. thesis submitted to the University of Western Australia, came to my attention as I was preparing the final draft of this chapter.

8. There is a passage in the *Short Treatise* in which Spinoza says that "up to now" only two of the attributes are known to us through their essence (*KV* I, vii, I:44), implying that the unknown attributes are not, in principle, unknowable. But his mature view seems to be that they are. See below.

9. Brunschvicg, *Spinoza et ses contemporains* (Paris: Felix Alcan, 1923), pp. 67–68.

10. However, the reference in the last sentence to "The point of view of absolute reality" seems to imply something with which I should not agree, namely, that there is no real difference between the attributes. This view of the attributes is not, I think, sustained by the evidence. On the whole, much discussed question see Francis Haserot, "Spinoza's Definition of Attribute," *Philosophical Review*, 62:499–513 (1953). Haserot's arguments seem to me quite conclusive and should put an end to the "subjective" interpretation of the attributes.

11. This would have to be the case because the complete description I speak

of is a set of propositions, where propositions are regarded not as linguistic entities but as a kind of universal *in rebus*.

12. Erik Stenius, *Wittgenstein's Tractatus* (Ithaca: Cornell University Press, 1960), p. 27.

13. Those who are struck by Tschirnhaus' use of the word *mundus* in this connection will be intrigued to know that he and Leibniz were very close friends.

14. This was argued by Pollock in *Spinoza: His Life and Philosophy* (London: C. K. Paul, 1880), p. 173. In the second edition (1899) Pollock is able to cite a letter of Leibniz that confirms his interpretation, p. 161.

15. The phrase is Pollock's, but he denies that this is all the doctrine of the infinite attributes amounts to, on the ground that it is "an extension of the parallelism already fixed in Spinoza's view of the world of human experience as a necessity of scientific thought" (2d ed., p. 158).

16. The classic study of this is Marjorie Nicolson's *The Microscope and the English Imagination* (Northampton, Mass., 1935). The bulk of this monograph has been reprinted in the author's *Science and Imagination* (Ithaca: Great Seal Books, 1956).

# Index